FLORENCE NIGHTINGALE
Founder of Modern Nursing

IMMORTALS OF HISTORY

FLORENCE NIGHTINGALE

Founder of Modern Nursing

by BARBARA HARMELINK

Franklin Watts, Inc.
575 Lexington Avenue
New York, N.Y. 10022

For my husband, Herman,
and my son, Alan, with
love

Cover photo courtesy The Bettmann Archive

Contents

Introduction

During her lifetime, Florence Nightingale, the founder of modern nursing, suffered from extravagant praise and extravagant blame. Sometimes she was called the sweetest, most tenderhearted woman alive, and sometimes she was said to be cold, ruthless, and quarrelsome. To the wounded soldiers of the Crimean War she was a saint, an angel sent from heaven with food and bandages, medicine, and clean bed linens. To the officers of the British Army Medical Department she was the devil, a wicked adventuress meddling in their affairs. Even if it is impossible for one small woman to be both saint and devil, the pendulum of Florence's life swung perilously close to both extremes.

Florence Nightingale's great adventure in the Crimean War lasted a brief two years. She was thirty-four years old before she was allowed to pour body and soul into the work to which she felt called by God. To answer this call, she gave up the man she might have married, and she rebelled against her outraged family, who expected her to enjoy the life of luxury for which they had trained her.

After the war was over, Florence was never the same again. The two years of overwork soon turned her into a permanent invalid. For nearly all the rest of her ninety years she lived in bed, working with her pen, and giving orders to her small group of devoted fellow workers. She founded her school of nursing without ever leaving her bedroom. She toiled in secret to help improve the lot of the British private soldier in England and in India. Her great sympathy for suffering people included the sick poor, and she worked to improve their medical care. She thought deeply about her religious beliefs and wrote several books on philosophy.

If Florence Nightingale could be called a saint, she was a reluctant one. She complained bitterly all the while she was sacrificing her life to the causes she believed in. Her barrage of self-pity drove away her friends and family, and she became a very unhappy woman.

Not until almost the end of her life could she find pleasure in what she had achieved. She mended the years-long quarrel with her family and enjoyed visits from relatives and nurses from her school. Warmed by their love, she could finally be happy that, at the turning point of her life, she had rejected marriage and chosen instead to lead the invasion of women nurses that turned the British Army Medical Department upside down.

BARBARA HARMELINK

FLORENCE
NIGHTINGALE
Founder of Modern Nursing

The Nightingales

Florence Nightingale's story began on May 12, 1820, when she was born in the Villa Colombaia, in Florence, Italy. She was baptized in the drawing room of the villa on July 4, by a clergyman of the Church of England. Her parents were enjoying a rather extended honeymoon in Italy, and were among the first English people to travel on the European continent after Napoleon's defeat at the Battle of Waterloo in 1815.

William and Frances Nightingale had been married in 1818, and their first daughter, Parthenope, was born in Naples the following year. (Parthenope was the Greek name for Naples.) The parents named both daughters for the towns where they were born, a fact that—in Parthenope's case—succeeded in startling people. The girls found their names hard to live with, so Parthenope became Parthe or Pop, and Florence became Flo.

The Nightingales were not particularly well-matched. William Edward Nightingale, W. E. N. to friends and family alike, had originally come from an old Derbyshire family called Shore. His prospects were rather bleak until, to his astonishment, he was named in the will of Peter Nightingale, his mother's uncle.

W. E. N. changed his name to Nightingale when he received his substantial inheritance in 1815. The money made possible a leisurely education at Edinburgh and Trinity College, Cambridge, and it also meant that he never had to settle down to earn a living. His inheritance cushioned him against reality for the rest of his life. In 1834, he decided to run for Parliament. He was enthusiastic about the reform of that body and had great dreams of a political career, but when he found that he could win only by bribing the electors he abruptly withdrew.

Nobody could understand why W. E. N. fell in love with Frances Smith.

The beautiful Fanny was six years older than he, as lively and vain as he was shy and studious. The Smiths were a large family, with five sons and five daughters who all lived for pleasure, much to their father's disgust. William Smith, like his father before him, was a distinguished philanthropist and public servant. He served his country for forty-six years as an unpaid member of Parliament, and for relaxation he collected paintings. When Fanny fell in love with a young man of good family but limited income, she tearfully renounced him because her father refused his permission for them to marry. Smith was too practical to allow his extravagant and luxury-loving daughter to marry without money, and he had too many other children to contemplate supporting her and a husband.

Brokenhearted, Fanny accepted W. E. N.'s proposal of marriage in 1817. She was thirty years old; he was twenty-four.

After their two-year honeymoon in Italy, they returned to England with their infant daughters and tried to settle down. W. E. N. had inherited a property in Derbyshire called Lea Hurst, but Fanny found the house too small, so they abandoned it and built a larger one. Still restless, she complained of the cold in the winter, so W. E. N. bought Embley Park, near Romsey in Hampshire, in the south of England. The house was large and elegant, set like a jewel in flower gardens and cultivated parkland.

Gradually the young family established a pattern of living: summer in Derbyshire, winter in Hampshire, and spring and autumn—the fashionable seasons—in London.

Fanny yearned for a London house, but she was content with the Burlington Hotel after it became obvious that W. E. N. would never enter Parliament or become a famous personality. So Fanny transferred her ambitions to her daughters, cultivating introductions that brought invitations to the "right" parties and keeping a sharp lookout for eligible suitors, even at this early stage.

The lack of a son was a serious matter in the Nightingale family. If W. E. N. did not produce a male child, the bulk of his fortune was to go to his sister's heir. Amid this potentially explosive situation, everybody behaved impeccably. W. E. N.'s sister, Mai, was cherished by Fanny, and by the girls whose future she threatened. When Mai married Fanny's brother Sam Smith, the rejoicing was genuine. The Smiths' son and heir was born when Florence was eleven years old. She was allowed to hold the infant in her arms, and she called him "my boy Shore." She adored him all her life, and when he grew up he loved her in return.

On the surface, life was as perfect for little Parthe and Flo as loving parents and wealth could make it. The family circle was wide, and cousins, aunts, and uncles were constantly visiting and writing back and forth. Besides cousins to play with, there were cats, dogs, and ponies, and houses and gardens with places to romp and corners to hide in. Parthe was a sunny and loving little girl who enjoyed life. She realized that Flo was more beautiful and gifted than she, and for many years Parthe was content to follow her younger sister's lead, even though she was puzzled by her.

While Parthe played, Flo developed a passion for wild flowers, which she industriously collected and cataloged. Her family offered her a variety of amusements but she steadfastly refused to be entertained by them.

From the age of six on, Florence was a problem. If she had been naughty she might have been easier to deal with. But she was not naughty—she was unhappy. Haunted by strange fancies, she was secretly terrified because she thought that she could not be like everyone else. Even her daydreams could not keep her from the knowledge that she hated the way in which she lived her life. Being rich and idle sickened her. She wanted a purpose in living, and her brilliant mind hungered for occupation.

The Nightingales differed sharply about their daughters' education. After much bickering, a Miss Christie was engaged to teach music and drawing. W. E. N. decided to be personally responsible for everything else. He self-consciously called the girls into his library where he set up an ambitious program for their formal education.

Fanny accepted the current nineteenth-century ideas and did not consider it either necessary or proper for young ladies to be highly educated. A girl should be able to write a letter, balance her household accounts, do fancy needlework, and be accomplished in drawing and music. That was sufficient. However, W. E. N. had other ideas.

Marriage to Fanny had not worked out in quite the way W. E. N. had expected. Therefore, he found solace in the company of his daughters. Extremely proud of their abilities, he was delighted to teach them philosophy, mathematics, Latin, and Greek. He shared with them his love for Italy, France, and Germany, and taught them the history and languages of those countries, as well as English history, language, and literature. Florence was the scholar, while Parthe, although able, succumbed to boredom and the temptation to escape and run errands for her mother.

As the girls grew, the seeds of a future family tragedy began to grow, too. More and more, Parthe yearned to be attractive and accomplished like her younger sister. Florence was the star even in the library, and Parthe could no longer stand it. As she grew more jealous, her jealousy began to poison the family. As for Florence, she could scarcely conceal her contempt for the life of domestic triviality for which she was destined. Inspired by the strong traditions of liberalism and philanthropy on both sides of her family, she grew more and more convinced that life and wealth had not been given to her for self-gratification, but in order to serve others.

Her relief and joy knew no bounds when, on February 7, 1837, she was "called by God." She described her "call" as coming at Embley in the form of a voice which she was convinced was the voice of God Himself. He asked her to serve Him, she said, but He did not say in what capacity. Yet, Florence was content to know that there was to be meaning in her life after all.

The "call" came in the midst of preparations for an extended tour of the Continent. Fanny had decided that it was almost time for the girls' debut, and Embley was too small for the kind of entertaining she had in mind. W. E. N. drew up plans for enlarging and altering the house, and he agreed with Fanny that it would be much more pleasant to visit Europe while the work was in progress.

Florence was a shy seventeen when the family sailed from Southampton on September 8, 1837. Nearly two years later, she would return, sophisticated and self-confident, to be presented to Queen Victoria.

Traveling was a delightful pastime for all the family. Secure in the knowledge that God would make her life significant, Florence forgot to be miserable in the bustle of boarding the big family coach, watching the scenery, and exploring famous churches, castles, and towns. Sight-seeing was interspersed with month-long stays at Nice and Genoa. W. E. N. had letters of introduction to prominent families in both France and Italy, and invitations were showered upon the young Misses Nightingale. They attended dances, picnics, and social gatherings, and basked in the attention of handsome young men. Leaving each place was agony, but the pain was soon drowned in the pleasures of the next town.

The Nightingales arrived in Florence on February 27, 1838, and settled at the Albergo del Arno near the Ponte Vecchio. In the city of her birth, Florence was able to enjoy two of her lifelong interests, music and politics. The opera was in full swing, and Florence devoted herself to it. She attended every possible performance, and kept copious notes in her travel diary about the librettos and scores, the artists, conductors, and composers.

In Florence, the young girl also became aware of the struggle for Italian freedom. W. E. N. was a supporter of the cause, and later that year Florence met some of the Italian exiles in Switzerland. She never forgot them. For years she sent money to help the Italian rebels, and on April 27, 1864, she would receive the Italian patriot Garibaldi at her home in London, at a time when she was too ill to see anybody except her closest friends and relatives.

Reluctantly, the Nightingales traveled north, through the Italian lake district, to Geneva where they spent most of September. W. E. N. could have settled there forever. Besides his social contacts, he had introductions at the university and he took Florence to meet the great scholars of the day, including Sismondi the historian.

Suddenly a political crisis erupted. Louis Napoleon Bonaparte, pretender to the throne of France, arrived in Geneva to visit his dying mother. The French king, Louis Philippe, demanded his expulsion, and the Swiss refused.

Florence was wild with excitement, and followed the debate in great detail.

The French moved their army up from Lyons to the Swiss border, and the people of Geneva erected barricades in the streets to stop the threatened invasion. At this point W. E. N. scooped up his precious family and made a dash

for Paris. Before they arrived the crisis was over. Louis
Napoleon was given a visa for England, and the French
withdrew their troops. Florence could not see the sense of
this at all. She guessed—correctly—that Louis Napoleon
was as great a menace in England as he was in Switzerland.
But in the meantime, life was fun, and the best was yet to
come in Paris.

The apartment which the Nightingales rented in the
French capital was splendid even by Fanny's standards.
Situated in the fashionable Place Vendôme, the windows
of the salon were draped in crimson satin and the furnishings included gilded mirrors and carved chairs.

Fanny's sister Patty had given her an introduction to a
Miss Mary Clark, who was one of the most sought-after
women in Paris. Clarkey, as the Nightingales affection-
ately came to call her, had had an unusual career. She had
risen from obscurity to become the presiding genius of a
"salon" in her house in the Rue du Bac. There, politicians
and men of letters conversed and read their works aloud,
in front of a few carefully chosen guests. Clarkey's recep-
tions included men such as Guizot, Thiers, Tocqueville,
Chateaubriand, and the gifted Madame Récamier.
W. E. N. and Fanny were delighted to be included in
such distinguished society, and they were proud of the way
Florence could hold her own in the conversations.

The winter in Paris sped away, and by April, 1839, the
family was back in London for the season. The Nightingales were charming people. They appeared to be a happy
family at the many social events they attended. But at
home total war was slowly developing.

CHAPTER

✠✠✠✠✠✠✠✠✠

II

✠✠✠✠✠✠✠✠✠

"The Two Nations"

Florence was the troublemaker in the Nightingale family. More and more, she felt compelled to do the direct opposite of what her parents wanted her to do.

On May 24, 1839, Queen Victoria's birthday, both Parthe and Florence were presented at court. Far from being impressed, when Florence wrote to Clarkey in Paris about the meeting, she devoted most of her letter to a political fracas called "The Bedchamber Plot." The new Tory prime minister, Sir Robert Peel, who had been in office only a few days, was forced to resign over a disagreement with the Queen concerning who should appoint her ladies-in-waiting. The Queen insisted that she would retain her Whig ladies-in-waiting. At the time, Queen Victoria was young and inexperienced, and Sir Robert did not know how to handle the situation. After the resignation, Lord William Melbourne, who had been prime minister before

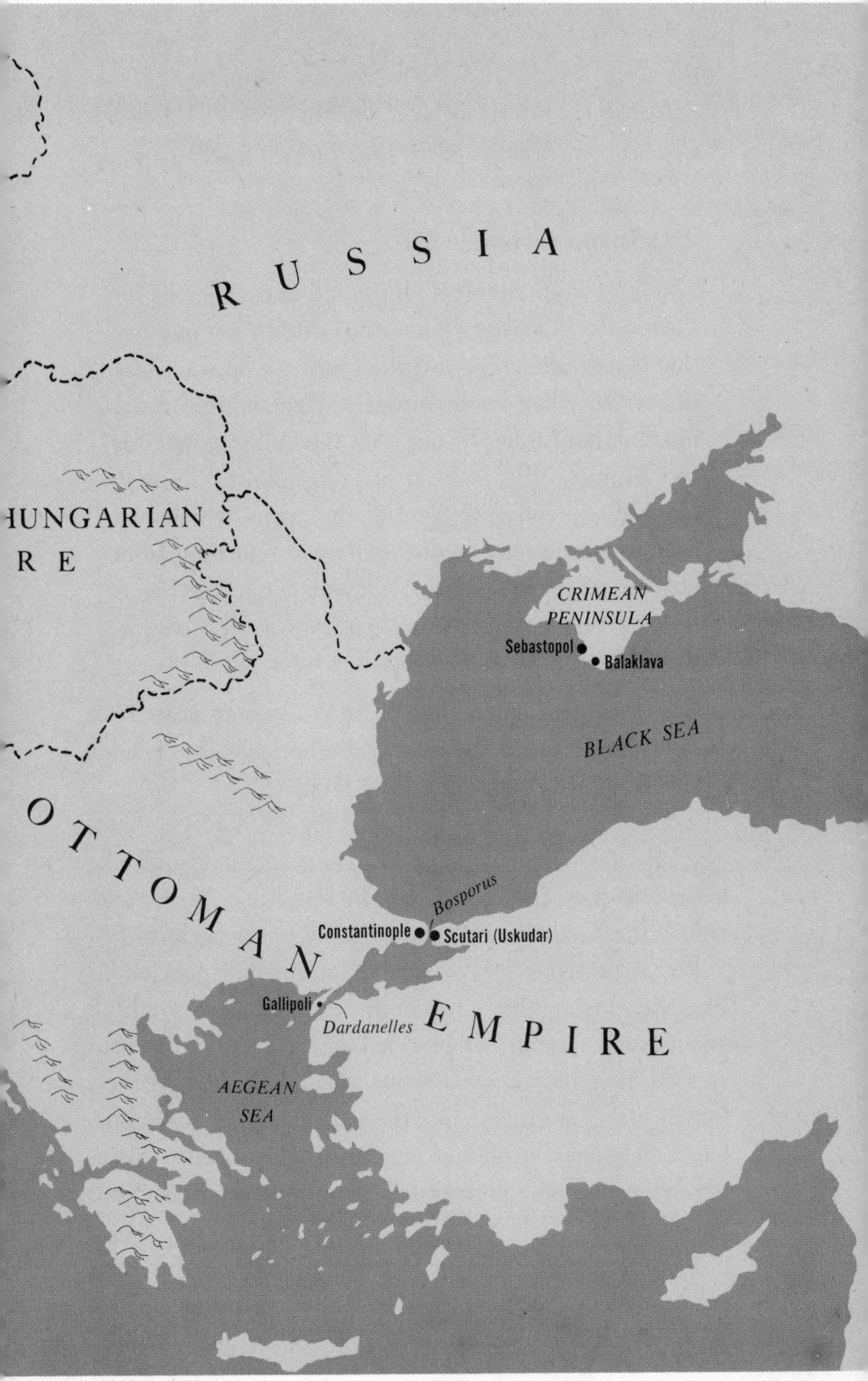

RUSSIA
HUNGARIAN
RE
CRIMEAN PENINSULA
Sebastopol
Balaklava
BLACK SEA
OTTOMAN EMPIRE
Bosporus
Constantinople
Scutari (Uskudar)
Gallipoli
Dardanelles
AEGEAN SEA

Sir Robert, was delighted to find himself back in power again.

To Clarkey, Florence wrote:

London was in a perfect whirlwind of excitement for the few days that the Melbourne ministry was out, but that is stale already. Our little Queen, who was sadly unpopular when we first came to England, recovered much of her former favour with the Whig party after the firmness she showed in this affair. She was cheered and called forward at the opera, which had not been done for months, and again returning from chapel. And the birthday drawing-room was over-flowing, whereas at the two first she gave this season, there were hardly forty people.

The letter was dated June 1, 1839. Twenty years later Florence and Queen Victoria would become close friends across the Queen's private dinner table.

The spirit of rebellion kept growing in Florence. Actually, she did not really want to rebel, and it would take her fourteen years to do it. Yet, she felt driven by her conviction that God had a special work for her to perform.

For a girl born to Florence Nightingale's position in England during the nineteenth century, even to think about work was an act of rebellion. Young ladies from wealthy families simply did not work. They obeyed their fathers until marriage, and then they obeyed their husbands. They could neither vote nor own property. Nothing was supposed to concern them beyond home and family.

By contrast, a girl born to a poor family at this time might work in a factory or a coal mine from the age of five.

She would be dirty and raggedly dressed, and half-starved as well. After marriage she would work until the last stages of pregnancy, and she would resume work as soon as she could take her child with her.

The gap between rich and poor was so wide that it seemed as if England was composed of two entirely separate nations. Benjamin Disraeli, one of the great statesmen of the nineteenth centry, wrote a book called *Sybil, or, The Two Nations*. In it, he described the cruel lot of the poor and the carelessness of the rich. (Florence noted in her diary that she had read a volume of *Sybil* aloud to her mother.)

The difference between the rich England and the poor England was most evident in the treatment of the sick. When a member of the Nightingale family fell ill, the word "hospital" was never even mentioned. A doctor was consulted and the patient stayed in bed at home. Nursing was usually left to the family and involved little more than keeping the patient company, ordering clean bed linens and nourishing foods, and giving the prescribed medicines.

The first significant contact that Florence had with the sick poor was in the village near the Nightingale estate in Derbyshire. During the wet summers of the 1840's, when the crops failed, Fanny occasionally allowed Florence to take food and medicines to the village people, who were victims of the countrywide starvation. When Florence witnessed the death of a woman in the village, she wrote to a cousin: "I saw a poor woman die before my eyes this summer because there was nothing but fools to sit up with her, who poisoned her as much as if they had given her arsenic."

The misery of the countrypeople was bad enough, but

the poor in the cities fared much worse. When there was
no one to care for them, the sick poor went to the same hospitals as did destitute people. An average hospital ward in
London in the 1840's was a sickening nightmare. Most
wards were long and narrow, crowded with about sixty
beds almost touching each other. The only source of heat
was a fireplace at one end, and since some hospitals
boarded up the windows to try and keep the heat in, there
was no fresh air. Walls usually streamed with moisture and
sometimes grew fungus. There seldom were adequate
bathroom facilities, so the patients used the floor.

After Florence became acquainted with hospital conditions, she would later write the following description:

> The nurses did not as a general rule wash patients,
> they could never wash their feet—and it was with
> difficulty and only in great haste that they could have
> a drop of water, just to dab their hands and face. The
> beds on which the patients lay were dirty. It was
> common practice to put a new patient into the same
> sheets used by the last occupant of the bed, and mat-
> tresses were generally of flock [cotton batting] sodden
> and seldom if ever cleaned.

Some of the patients took to drink as relief from the pain
and horror of the hospitals. It was not unknown for fights
to break out in the wards, and the metropolitan police—
London's famous "Bobbies," founded by Sir Robert Peel in
1829—were often called in. Their job was to stop the
patients from killing each other.

It was the practice to hire as nurses women who had
borne children out of wedlock. Some of them were prosti-

tutes. The nurses were not much better off than the patients and generally lived in the wards, cooking their own food and sleeping there, often alone and unsupervised. Some practiced prostitution in the wards, and nearly all of them drank heavily. Medical training was negligible.

The Nightingales were aware of this human misery, but they accepted it as a necessary evil. As churchgoers, they had listened to the biblical directives to feed the hungry, aid the sick, and visit the imprisoned. In fairness, they did what they thought was expected of them. They were extraordinarily kind to their servants and dependents, and Fanny was famous for her generosity toward the village people. However, she refused Florence sharply when the young girl badgered her for more food and medicines for distribution.

Fortunately for Florence, and for those in need, there were some members of the rich nation who cared about their fellow Englishmen. In 1840, the Nightingales were invited to dinner by a new neighbor, Lord Palmerston. Seated at the table was one of the most distinguished young noblemen in England, Lord Ashley (Anthony Ashley Cooper, later the 7th Earl of Shaftesbury). This young man exercised a powerful influence over Florence for many years. She was thrilled beyond description by the conversation and correspondence of a wealthy man who devoted his life and his possessions to the improvement of the conditions of the poor.

From Lord Ashley, Florence learned the full extent of the poor's misery. Lord Ashley was particularly concerned about working conditions in the coal mines. In 1840, the trade union movement had scarcely been born, so improvements did not come from the wealthy, who were represented in Parliament, they would not come at all. Lord Ashley made an investigation into the mines, and wrote a bill for Parliament which became the Mines Act of 1842. The Mines Act prohibited the employment of women and children underground, and provided for government inspection of the mines. Since the mineowners feared the inspectors, they were forced to introduce better safety measures, and as a result many accidents were prevented. The owners hated Lord Ashley, because their profits declined with the loss of slave labor and the need for spending money on improvements.

Lord Ashley worked to help the poor in the factories that were being built in England as a result of the Industrial Revolution. He also worked to improve the hospitals and the health of the nation. In Florence, he found an eager pupil. As she grew steadily more convinced that she had been called by God to help the poor, she turned to Lord Ashley for information. He supplied her with blue books (government reports) on working-class conditions, and he added reports on hospitals to the list as Florence became definite about her desire to train as a nurse.

In the meantime, W. E. N. and Fanny had great hopes for Florence's future. They pictured her as the mistress of a large country mansion, and presiding over the best parties of the London season. They planned to find her a kind and wealthy husband, and wished her the joy of little children. However, their youngest daughter had other ideas.

✢✢✢✢✢✢✢✢✢

III

✢✢✢✢✢✢✢✢✢

The Fight

As Florence began to realize the privations of the poor, her personal life was slowly being ruined. Although she trembled at the price of self-sacrifice, she was more and more driven to cast off her home and family. She drew closer to the relatives who would help her, and she made friends who encouraged her to come to a decision about her future.

For the Christmas holidays in 1841, the Nightingales, as usual, visited the Nicholson family in Surrey. Marianne Nicholson, the daughter of Fanny's sister Anne, was one of Florence's best friends. There were eighty people sleeping in the house that Christmas, enough to cast a full-scale production of "The Merchant of Venice." Parthe was the scene painter and helped with the costumes, while Florence was the stage manager, and helped the actors to learn their lines. The young people also danced and played games, and the climax of the festivities was a masked ball which lasted until five o'clock in the morning.

Florence had developed a kind of obsession about Marianne Nicholson. The two girls were inseparable, and they enjoyed each other's company during the London seasons, as well as during the holidays. Unfortunately, Marianne's brother Henry complicated their friendship. He fell in love with Florence, and because she wanted to be with Marianne she unintentionally encouraged Henry. The Nightingales and the Nicholsons were delighted at the thought of their children marrying each other, but Florence knew that she did not care for Henry.

Florence also spent a good deal of the time with another member of the Nicholson family, Aunt Hannah, when she was visiting in Surrey. When they were apart, Florence wrote long letters to her. Aunt Hannah was a saintly woman who assumed the responsibility for Florence's religious instruction. Her advice was helpful for a while, but Florence felt that it did not go far enough. Aunt Hannah kept telling her to obey her parents, and Florence became more and more certain that in order to serve God she would have to rebel against them. The relationship ended abruptly when Aunt Hannah refused to see Florence or write to her, declaring that she was undutiful.

But Aunt Mai was far more understanding. She sensed the restlessness and loneliness in Florence. She encouraged her to study and tried to protect her from her mother's ambitions. But in March, 1842, the Nightingales went to London for the season, as usual, and stayed, as usual, at the Burlington Hotel. Despite her restlessness, Florence could not help enjoying herself, perhaps because she was only twenty-two.

In London, Florence met the Prussian Ambassador (the Chevalier Bunsen) and his wife, who took a fancy to her. She could go to their house at any time to talk, and they paid her the compliment of taking seriously her desire to help mankind. Fanny was pleased that her daughter was liked by personal friends of Queen Victoria and Prince Albert.

The Bunsens were enormously rich, and lived on a grand scale in Carlton House Terrace, and on an estate in Sussex. Yet, these were the people who actually gave Florence the idea of taking nurses' training. They told her of one German pastor's attempt to help the destitute by founding a hospital, the Institution of Deaconesses at Kaiserwerth, near Düsseldorf, Germany.

In May, the Nightingales returned to Embley to prepare for the summer at Lea Hurst. Soon after, they were once again invited to a dinner party by Lord Palmerston. This time Florence met Richard Monckton Milnes. He was highly eligible, and soon he was very much in love with Florence. Thirty-three, handsome, wealthy, intelligent, and famous, he might have been a perfect husband for Florence. His special interest was juvenile delinquency, and he worked to keep youngsters from jail and the company of criminals by putting them into reformatories. Besides his political career he had a taste for poetry. He "discovered" the poet Keats and arranged for the first book of his poems to be published. Fanny could see that this was a far better match than Henry Nicholson, and she openly encouraged it.

Although the world lay at Florence's feet, something about it disturbed her deeply. She wrote in her diary: "My mind is absorbed with the idea of the sufferings of man, it besets me behind and before. . . ." As the starvation in England grew worse, Florence became more and more nervous and upset, and the more she attended lavish parties, dances, and dinners, the more they disgusted her. At times, even Marianne disgusted her, and she felt that her only true friend was another cousin, Hilary Bonham-Carter.

Things continued in much the same manner until the Christmas holidays of 1843, when Florence had a nervous collapse. She spent the holidays at Surrey in bed, too distraught to join in the fun. She was tempted to marry Richard, but she was terrified that marriage would prevent her from fulfilling what she felt to be her destiny. Somehow she would have to nurse the sick. By spring of the following year, she had made up her mind—her only problem was how an English lady could become a nurse.

At first, Florence imagined herself in the role of a lady visitor, laying a cooling hand on feverish foreheads. But several events in 1845 changed her mind. In February of that year, she nursed her nephew Shore, who was suffering from measles. In March, Henry Nicholson proposed to her, and she refused him. The Nicholsons were outraged and broke off relations with the Nightingales. Marianne was particularly bitter, and never really forgave Florence even when the two families later made up their quarrel. Five years after Florence refused Henry, he drowned while on vacation in Spain.

During the rest of 1845, Florence had more nursing experience. She nursed her grandmother Mrs. Shore in August, and her old nurse, Mrs. Gale, immediately afterward. Mrs. Gale died while Florence was holding her hand, and the young woman was so upset that she went flying to her mother for comfort. But her distress changed to anger at her own incompetence, and slowly she evolved a plan.

Dr. Fowler, a friend of the family, was the head physician at the Salisbury Infirmary near Embley. In December, 1845, Florence worked up enough courage to announce to her family that she would go to the infirmary and study for three months under Dr. Fowler's care. She was going to become a nurse.

Her father, mother, and sister went into hysterics. She might just as well have told them that she intended to live in a brothel. The Fowlers, who happened to be guests at Embley when Florence made her announcement, were dreadfully embarrassed to be caught in the family crossfire. W. E. N. soon rushed off to London because he could not stand all his women crying and quarreling and "taking leave of their senses." Fanny accused Florence of having an illicit love affair with a surgeon. Parthe felt betrayed. She had basked in Florence's reflected glory, and now there was nothing left to live for.

After hours of hysterical recriminations, Florence was forced to abandon her idea. But from this time on, she was set on a course that would drive her out of the family circle.

Florence refused to give up. This girl who was always too fatigued to carry out the simplest household duties now began getting up hours before breakfast and studying by candlelight. She read everything that Lord Ashley could send her, and before the end of 1846, she was an expert on hospital conditions, sanitation, and public health. Clarkey also sent her everything she could find in Paris, and the Bunsens sent material from Berlin. Along with the Bunsens' reports and books came the yearbook of the Institution of Deaconesses at Kaiserwerth. Here was a place where a respectable lady could be trained as a nurse without entering a public hospital or taking the drastic step of becoming a Roman Catholic nun.

Because her family continued to oppose her, Florence became seriously ill. She hovered on the brink of a mental breakdown, and retreated into a dreamworld.

Charles and Selina Bracebridge, sympathetic friends of the Nightingale family, realized that Florence had to get away. They proposed a holiday, and in October of 1847, Florence was persuaded to get out of bed and leave with them for Rome. Safely removed from family conflict, she recovered almost immediately, and a significant part of that recovery was due to some new friends.

In Rome, Florence met Sidney and Elizabeth (Liz) Herbert, who were on their honeymoon. Sidney, later Lord Herbert of Lea, had served in Sir Robert Peel's administration as head of the Admiralty. He was an ardent reformer like his colleague Lord Ashley, and was especially interested in reforming hospital conditions. The Herberts were thrilled at Florence's idea of becoming a nurse, and they promised to help her when they returned to England.

By April, 1848, the vacationers were home in London. But once she was reunited with her family, Florence became just as ill as before. Her parents refused to understand. The idea of her being a nurse made them irate. She would disgrace them, and they closed their minds to the opinions of men such as Lord Ashley or Sidney Herbert.

They would not change their minds even for the Bunsens, who were considering sending their own daughter to Kaiserwerth. W. E. N. was so disgusted that he had as little to do with his family as possible, and Fanny and Parthe both treated Florence cruelly.

At this point in her life, when escape from her family was a desperate need, Richard Monckton Milnes proposed to Florence and insisted that she give him an answer. She refused him, but the decision was so difficult that he haunted her memory for years. The news that he later married someone else was a great blow to her.

Once again the Bracebridges came to the rescue. They obtained permission to take Florence with them to Egypt, but the trip did nothing to improve her health. As a last resort, Selina Bracebridge took the matter into her own hands. Without the Nightingales' knowledge or permission, she arranged their return journey overland and left Florence at Kaiserwerth, in Germany. Florence spent the first two weeks of August, 1850, working every nerve and muscle in her body. Yet, as if by a miracle, she was restored to glowing health.

Kaiserwerth had been founded in 1833 by Theodor Fliedner and his wife. The institution had grown from shelter offered to one destitute ex-convict to a one-hundred-bed hospital, with an infant school, penitentiary, orphan asylum, and a normal school for training teachers. Florence reveled in the crude physical conditions and frugal meals, and the spoken prayers that preceded every activity of the day. She later wrote an exhaustive thirty-two-page report on the institution, which was published in 1851.

At the end of the month she came home and spent about two happy hours with her family. That was how long it took for them to discover where she had been, and they were beside themselves with fury. W. E. N. and Fanny agreed that she should be punished. In return for her expensive holiday, she would be required to devote the next six months entirely to her sister.

Matters were now becoming ridiculous. Florence was thirty years old, not a naughty child, and Parthe was not cured of her jealousy by having Florence as her slave. So, Fanny gave way in the end and took both daughters to Carlsbad, Germany, in the summer of 1851. Parthe took the cure there and Florence, in secrecy, began to work at Kaiserwerth. When Florence poured out her heart to her mother and sister in a long letter from the hospital, trying to explain what she was doing, they did not reply. They absolutely refused to accept any explanation, and for Florence this was finally the end of her family life. She decided to leave home at the earliest opportunity.

Yet two more years of captivity remained, and they were the most painful. Florence almost decided to become a nun, but was finally dissuaded by her adviser, Cardinal Manning. The Cardinal realized that this would not be a genuine conversion, so he arranged instead for permission for Florence to study with the Sisters of Charity in Paris, a nursing order. But before she could go, W. E. N. fell ill and she stayed home to nurse him.

Florence was on the point of leaving in 1852, when Parthe had a serious nervous breakdown. She was attended by the Queen's physician, Sir James Clark, who made his opinion quite clear: Parthe's only chance of a normal life was to live without Florence, whose presence deeply upset her. At last Florence really felt free to go.

Fanny made one more desperate attempt to keep her. She offered to give Florence a large country house, recently left to Fanny by an aunt. Florence could establish and run her own hospital and train her own nurses at Fanny's expense. But the offer had come too late. Florence packed and went to stay with Clarkey in Paris for a month, prior to entering the convent of the Sisters of Charity.

Fanny gave her permission for the Paris trip while deluding herself that Florence needed to buy dresses there, but Florence never came home again. Grandmother Shore's last illness sent her hurrying back to England to nurse her. After the old lady's death, Florence went to London to be interviewed for a job that was suggested by Liz Herbert. The position was superintendent of the Institution for the Care of Sick Gentlewomen in Distressed Circumstances. She would receive no payment and would be responsible for her own expenses and those of a matron, who was to be her chaperone.

After her family learned of this interview, a reunion was unthinkable. W. E. N. declared that he could not endure one more scene, and left once again for his London club. He decided to give Florence her independence and an income of five hundred pounds a year. Free at last, Florence returned to Paris and entered the nursing order, only to catch measles and have her plans thwarted once again. She recovered at Clarkey's house, and returned to London where she began her job as superintendent. On August 12, 1853, she moved into the institution's new headquarters at 1 Harley Street, to begin her career as a nurse.

Florence Nightingale was thirty-three years old. In order to protect herself against her family's fury through the years, she had become proud, cold, and ruthlessly ambitious. She stood on a lonely pinnacle, a clever woman determined to work, in an age which condemned rich women to idleness.

CHAPTER

✦✦✦✦✦✦✦✦✦

IV

✦✦✦✦✦✦✦✦✦

The Way to Turkey

Aunt Mai helped Florence to move into the headquarters on Harley Street and prepare for her first patients. At last, Florence was free from family obligations. In fact, her family seemed to find her much easier to love at a distance, and Fanny began to shower her with gifts. From Embley came old washed and mended bed sheets, unwanted household items, special food, and boxes of fresh flowers to cheer the patients.

Florence did everything in her power to heal and comfort her sick gentlewomen. Her concept of nursing included good administration as well as good medical care, and no detail escaped her. She personally supervised everything from the cleaning of kitchen closets to the reorganizing of the bookkeeping. Most of the staff left immediately, of course, but Florence cheerfully accepted their resignations and appointed replacements more to her liking. She

had no use for the "lady" nurse who was too grand to get
her hands dirty. The kind of woman she wanted to train
had to be prepared to wash patients, bedding, and floors.
Very little was understood at that time about sanitation and
the communication of diseases, but Florence insisted upon
cleanliness and fresh air as part of caring for the sick.

Each patient received special treatment. Class distinc-
tion meant nothing to Florence. These women were
human beings in need and she cared for all their needs,
not just their sick bodies. She wrote to their families, found
them jobs, arranged short vacations at her own expense,
and sometimes she gave them her own money. She loved
them like a mother, and in return they worshiped her.

Florence was a much different woman when it came to
dealing with the committee that governed the institution.
The committee was composed of both ladies and gentle-
men, who met separately, and they were all very nervous
about making any decisions. Liz Herbert was Florence's
ally on the ladies' committee, and she carefully explained
Florence's ideas on how the institution should be run. But
Florence played a shrewd game of politics herself. She
went to work on the ladies, winning them over one by one
by demonstrating her excellent management. She flattered
and cajoled them, and surreptitiously fed them her schemes,
which they could then produce at the next committee
meeting, as if they had just thought of them. The system
was devious, but it worked.

Florence soon described the Harley Street institution as
"this little mole hill." In a few months she had everything
running smoothly, and the job began to bore her. With the
help of Sidney and Liz Herbert, she started to look around

for something more exciting. Sidney was deeply committed
to the reform of the hospitals, and he realized that without
decent nurses a cleaner building would mean little. Nor
would it stay clean for very long. The three of them were
working on a scheme for Florence to start a nurses' training
program designed to attract respectable women, when war
broke out in the East.

The Crimean War, which saw an uneasy alliance of
Britain and France pitted against the Imperial Russian
Army, lasted from 1854 to 1856. It was an angry flare-up
in a series of troubles concerning the future of the Turkish
Empire, which had its capital at Constantinople. The outbreak of hostilities was provoked by Louis Napoleon Bonaparte, now emperor of France. He was employing a well-
known stratagem by seeking a glorious war abroad to dis-
tract people from hard times at home.

The city of Jerusalem was part of the Turkish Empire,
and it was a holy place for the Muslims as well as for Jews
and Christians. The sultan of Turkey naturally gave pref-
erence to the Muslims when they asked for special protec-
tion for their mosques, although he grudgingly allowed
the Christians to care for the Church of the Holy Sepulchre. French monks from the Roman Catholic Church had
celebrated Mass there until the atheistic rule of Napoleon
the Great. When the church was neglected, Russian
monks from the Eastern Orthodox Church took over.
Louis Napoleon decided to revive the French monks'
claim to a set of keys to the church. By this step, he hoped
to appear devout to the Roman Catholics in France, and he
also hoped to provoke the Russians. Everything went according to plan and the czar of Russia, Nicholas I, for-

bade the sultan to hand over a duplicate set of the keys.

The British quarrel with Russia was more serious. The czar was seeking commercial enterprises to the south, as far afield as Afghanistan, and everywhere he tried to gain influence, he challenged British interests. The Russian problem was that all her major seaports were frozen solid during the winter, with the exception of Sebastopol (now Sevastopol), on the Crimean peninsula in the Black Sea. But Sebastopol had a serious disadvantage, too. There was no exit from the Black Sea except right through the heart of Constantinople, the city which guarded the passage through the Dardanelles. The czar was constantly looking for an excuse to break up the Turkish Empire and seize Constantinople; the British were equally determined that he should do no such thing.

The sultan of Turkey was well aware of his perilous position. Caught between Russian and French demands for the rights to the Church of the Holy Sepulchre, he turned for advice to the British ambassador, Lord Stratford de Redcliffe. Neither Lord Stratford nor Lord Palmerston agreed with England's official policy of extreme caution in regard to Russia, and they saw this quarrel as an opportunity to humiliate the czar.

Lord Stratford advised the sultan to insist that the czar hand over the keys. When Nicholas threatened to invade Turkey, Lord Stratford called the Russian's bluff and told the sultan to stand firm. However, the czar was not bluffing. The Russians invaded Turkey; Britain was drawn into a senseless war that cost the lives of 600,000 men, and resulted in no permanent change in the Eastern situation.

In fact, when the terms of the peace settlement were discussed in Paris two years later, the keys to the church were not even mentioned.

In 1854, Sidney Herbert was England's Secretary at War and, as such, was responsible for finances. His senior was the Duke of Newcastle, Secretary for War, who was responsible for the armed forces.

The British army had last seen action forty years before, in the victory over Napoleon at the Battle of Waterloo. Since that time every aspect of the army had deteriorated. The Duke of Wellington, who had led the army at Waterloo, had been resting on his laurels, continuing to head the army long after his usefulness had ceased. Nobody had dared to contradict him, even though the administration had fallen into chaos and the battalions had not been maintained at full strength. Herbert had to shoulder the blame despite the fact that he had not held office long enough to achieve any results. And although he worked diligently to strengthen the army, British public opinion could not forgive him for having a Russian mother and an uncle with a palace at Yalta in the Crimea, near the scene of most of the fighting.

The Army Medical Department was perpetually understaffed. A wounded officer did receive some scant medical attention, but the common soldier was pretty much ignored. There were not enough surgeons to tend to the men, and women nurses were not permitted near the troops because of their scandalous reputation. This was how it had always been, and the army doctors never expected it to get any better. They were particularly outraged at public reaction to letters sent to *The Times* of London

by William Howard Russell, special correspondent assigned to the Crimean War.

The Times correspondents were pioneers in the field of
reporting, and this was the first time that people were able
to read a newspaperman's comments on the conduct of a
war while it was actually being fought. Russell denounced
the inefficiency of the army's methods of treating the sick
and wounded. In a letter published on October 9, he declared that since there were no nurses the wounded soldiers had to help each other. On October 12, The Times
published a blistering attack on the Army Medical Department written from Constantinople.

It is with feelings of surprise and anger that the
public will learn that no sufficient preparations have
been made for the proper care of the wounded. Not
only are there not sufficient surgeons—that, it might
be urged, was unavoidable; not only are there no
dressers and nurses—that might be a defect of system
for which no one is to blame, but what will be said
when it is known that there is not even linen to make
bandages for the wounded? . . . And yet, after the
troops have been six months in the country, there is
no preparation for the commonest surgical operation! Not only are the men kept, in some cases, for a
week without the hand of a medical man coming near
their wounds; not only are they left to expire in
agony, unheeded and shaken off, though catching
desperately at the surgeon whenever he makes his
rounds through the fetid ship; but now, when they
are placed in the spacious building, where we were

led to believe that everything was ready which could ease their pain or facilitate their recovery, it is found that the commonest appliances of a workhouse sick-ward are wanting, and that the men must die through the Medical Staff of the British army having forgotten that old rags are necessary for the dressing of wounds. If Parliament were sitting, some notice would prob-ably be taken of these facts, which are notorious and have excited much concern; as it is, it rests with the Government to make inquiries into the conduct of those who have so greatly neglected their duty.

Russell was referring to the *Kangaroo,* one of the hos-pital ships that transported the wounded from the battle-fields of the Crimea to the barracks of the Turkish army at Scutari (modern Usküdar).

The Scutari barracks, on the Asian shores of the Bos-phorus (Bosporus), just across from Constantinople, had been assigned to the British for use as a hospital because the General Hospital nearby, which had nine hundred beds, overflowed with sick and wounded soldiers. Russell wrote another letter complaining that the French army had much better arrangements for their wounded, including the services of the Sisters of Charity.

The Times appealed to its readers for money and gifts to help the soldiers, and the response was overwhelming. A man named Macdonald was put in charge of the collection, and he soon left for the Middle East. One of the first questions asked by a stunned British public was why their army had no Sisters of Charity. It was the opening that Herbert had been looking for. He immediately wrote to

Florence asking her to lead a party of nurses and break the army's prejudice against women.

As it turned out, Florence had already made plans to go to Scutari on her own, but now she could go in an official capacity.

In Herbert's detailed letter, he told Florence why she should go to the war. She should not go only to minister to wounded men, but to prove that nurses could behave like ladies, and could serve without friction within the framework of the Army Medical Department.

> The selection of the rank and file of nurses will be very difficult: no one knows it better than yourself. The difficulty of finding women equal to a task, after all, full of horrors, and requiring, besides knowledge and goodwill, great energy and great courage, will be great. The task of ruling them and introducing system among them, great; and not the least will be the difficulty of making the whole work smoothly with the medical and military authorities out there.

Neither Herbert nor Florence could foresee the violent hatred that their scheme would arouse among the medical men.

In choosing Florence to introduce female nursing into the army, Herbert had selected the right woman. She would achieve far more than they hoped.

Herbert rushed to obtain government sanction for his idea, and on October 19, 1854, he wrote to Florence in his official capacity:

> Madam—Having consented at the pressing instance of the Government to accept the office of Superin-

tendent of the female nursing establishment in the
English General Military Hospitals in Turkey, you
will, on your arrival there, place yourself at once in
communication with the Chief Army Medical Officer
of the Hospital at Scutari, under whose orders and
direction you will carry on the duties of your appointment.

The letter also contained detailed instructions concerning the selection of nurses, and applications for money to
meet all the expenses of the expedition.

It took Florence exactly four days to choose her party,
equip them, and leave. Her calmness in the face of this
gigantic task was remarkable to everyone but herself. After
all, this was the moment for which she had been preparing
herself most of her life.

Herbert was understandably worried about obtaining
the Nightingales' permission for their daughter to leave
on this unusual adventure. The Bracebridges decided to go
with her, and Sam Smith, Aunt Mai's husband, was
elected to explain to the Nightingales why they should
give their consent. But persuasion was not necessary.
W. E. N. and Fanny were astonished and flattered that the
government should request their daughter's services. They
were so pleased at the sensation the appointment caused
that they rushed up to London to see her off.

Even Parthe felt good about it and wrote warmly to a
friend:

Before, in Harley Street, I did not feel sure that she was
right, there seemed so much to be done at home; but
now there is no doubt that she is fitted to do this work,

and that no one else is, and that it *is* a work. I must
say the way in which all things have tended to and
fitted her for this is so very remarkable that one cannot but believe she was intended for it. None of her
previous life has been wasted, her experience all tells,
all the gathered stores of so many years, her Kaiserwerth, her sympathy with the R. Catholic system of
work, her travels, her search into the hospital question, her knowledge of so many different minds and
different classes, all are serving so curiously . . .

It was ironic that the very thing that the Nightingales
feared would disgrace them—namely Florence's becoming
a nurse—would bring them honor and fame. Neither
Fanny nor Parthe could stand the idea of what Florence
did, but national applause helped them to overcome some
of their aversion. At least they now became sympathetic.
Liz Herbert obtained Florence's release from the institution in Harley Street, and offered the Herbert town house
for the expedition's headquarters.

Choosing hospital nurses was the hardest part of all.
Selina Bracebridge helped Florence to select them from
the drab bunch of women who applied at the front door of
the Herberts' house in Belgrave Square. The whole group
finally numbered thirty-eight, of whom only fourteen were
regular hospital nurses. The other nurses were Roman
Catholic and Anglican nuns. Each woman signed a paper
agreeing that she would accept the absolute authority of
Miss Nightingale. Through the intervention of Cardinal
Manning, the Roman Catholic nuns were given permission to do this, and Florence had to insist upon it. Any
nurse who disobeyed her was subject to instant dismissal.

Florence believed in the value of nursing, and she was willing to give her life to make it an honorable profession in the face of indifference, scorn, and violent opposition. She knew that her mission would fail if any of her party disobeyed the military authorities, or if there was any scandal involving her nurses. She also had to protect the nurses from the army. The nuns would wear their habits, and a specially designed uniform was provided for the others. The dresses were shapeless, made of gray wool, with a jacket and cloak of similar material. The women wore plain white caps on their heads, and scarves around their necks with the words "Scutari Hospital" embroidered in red. In these costumes, they could not be confused with camp prostitutes. They were paid a small amount each week, with food, lodging, and uniform provided.

Everything was ready when the group was due to leave on the morning of Saturday, October 21, 1854. Florence carried with her a small black pocketbook with three letters inside.

One was from her mother, who wrote: "Monday morning. God speed you on your errand of mercy, my own dearest child. I know He will, for He has given you such loving friends, and they will be always at your side to help in all your difficulties. . . ."

Richard Monckton Milnes had written: "I hear you are going to the East. . . . You can undertake that, when you could not undertake me. God bless you, dear friend, wherever you go."

Cardinal Manning had committed her to God's care: "God will keep you," he wrote, "and my prayer for you will be that your one object of Worship, Pattern of Imitation, and Source of consolation and strength may be the Sacred Heart of our Divine Lord."

Just before Florence left for the East, she was described by the English novelist Elizabeth Gaskell, as follows:

> . . . She is tall; very slight and willowy in figure; thick shortish rich brown hair; very delicate coloring; grey eyes which are generally pensive and drooping, but which when they choose can be the merriest eyes I ever saw. Put a long piece of soft net, say 1¼ yards long and half a yard wide, and tie it round this beautifully shaped head, so as to form a soft white framework for the full oval of her face (for she had the toothache and so wore this little piece of drapery) and dress her up in black silk high up to the long white round throat, and a black shawl on and you may get NEAR an idea of her perfect grace and lovely appearance. . . . She has a great deal of fun and is carried along by that I think. She mimics most capitally. . . .

Mrs. Gaskell had been a guest at Lea Hurst when Florence was taking a few days' vacation from Harley Street, and that was her first impression of the beautiful socialite. And that is how Florence is pictured in history, too, as a lovely lady in black silk, tending the suffering soldiers.

But Florence had another side, as Mrs. Gaskell discovered much to her chagrin:

> She has no friend—and she wants none. She stands perfectly alone, halfway between God and his creatures. She used to go a great deal among the villagers

here who dote upon her. One poor woman lost a boy
seven years ago of white swelling in his knee, and
F. N. went twice a day to dress it. . . . The mother
speaks of F. N.—did so to me only yesterday—as of a
heavenly angel. Yet the father of this dead child—the
husband of this poor woman—died last 5th of September and I was witness to the extreme difficulty
with which Parthe induced Florence to go and see
this childless widow ONCE whilst she was here; and
though this woman entreated her to come again, she
never did. She will not go among the villagers now
because her heart and soul are absorbed by her hospital plans, and, as she says, she can only attend to
one thing at once. She is so excessively gentle in voice,
manner and movement, that one never feels the un-
bendableness of her character when one is near her.
Her powers are astonishing. . . .

Florence had already demonstrated her powers in her
management of the committee of the Harley Street institution. She was single-minded in pursuit of her beliefs and
was able to disregard things that were irrelevant to her
purpose. The British Army Medical Department would
soon learn just how single-minded she could be.

CHAPTER

✳✳✳✳✳✳✳✳✳

V

✳✳✳✳✳✳✳✳✳

Into Battle

With Uncle Sam Smith playing escort as far as Marseilles in the south of France, Florence and her nurses set out for Constantinople. They spent their first night away from home in Boulogne. When they got off the cross-channel steamer they were astonished to find themselves famous. Many of the inhabitants of Boulogne had sons or fathers fighting with the French army in the Crimea. They shouted names and messages at the bewildered Englishwomen, seized their bags, and carried the ladies off to the local hotel where they were treated as royalty and not charged for anything.

Trouble flared up immediately. At dinner the other women in the party refused to eat with the hospital nurses. Florence got up and waited on each one of the nurses in turn, since none of them could speak French. When they had all been served she drew up a chair and ate with the

nurses herself. The effect that she had on these rough
women was extraordinary. Their table manners improved
as if by magic, and so did their language. In one of his
letters, Sam Smith reported hearing one say to another:
" 'We never had so much care taken of our comforts before;
it is not people's way with *us*; we had no notion Miss N.
would slave herself so for us.' "

In Marseilles, Florence received a group of merchants
from whom she bought quantities of food and several
portable cooking stoves. She had been told by Dr. Andrew
Smith, the Chief Army Medical Officer in London, that
the hospitals in Turkey had everything she needed, but
she had not believed him. Uncle Sam helped to stow all
the supplies on board the *Vectis*, and then waved the party
good-bye.

It was a stormy passage, and Florence was seasick most
of the time, too ill even to be bothered by the numerous
cockroaches. The *Vectis* made one stop at Malta. Florence
could not move from her bed, so an embarrassed major
escorted some of the party ashore. He lined them up like
soldiers, with the black-clad Anglican nuns in front. He
placed the hospital nurses in the middle to keep them out
of mischief, and some of the Roman Catholic nuns,
dressed in white, brought up the rear. Confusion reigned
as the women were soon followed by a gaping crowd of
soldiers stationed on the island. "Forward black sisters,"
the major shouted. And then, "Halt! Those damned white
sisters have gone again," as nuns and nurses began to dis-
appear from his view. He rounded them up at last and they
went back on board for the remainder of the journey to
Constantinople.

The first engagement of the Crimean War had been fought in April. H.M.S. *Furious,* a British naval steamer, had been sent to Odessa to collect the British consul. Odessa was a fashionable seaside town, with harbor facilities second only to Sebastopol in the Black Sea. The Russians fired on the rowboat bearing the message for the consul, and the British retaliated by bringing up the navy and bombarding the town.

It took the British army four months to travel to Constantinople following the same route that took Florence two weeks. The main body camped in Scutari, using the Turkish barracks as headquarters. The French army had its headquarters at Gallipoli. The respective commanders, Lord Raglan and Marshal St.-Arnaud, were unable to come to any agreement as to where the war should be fought, and while they dithered with diplomatic niceties the Russian army was slowly advancing through Bulgaria to threaten Constantinople. The Russians were driven back by the Turkish army with the help of two British officers, and at this point the war should have come to an end. When the British and French finally got around to landing their forces in Bulgaria they never made contact with the enemy. However, the men suffered cruelly from the heat and from lack of food and shelter. They were also stricken by an epidemic of cholera. The sick were sent across the Black Sea to Scutari where the General Hospital was soon overflowing. That is why the Turkish barracks were handed over to the British for use as a temporary hospital.

Early in September the armies had embarked from Varna, in Bulgaria, to cross the Black Sea for the invasion of the Crimean peninsula. The only reason given for this extraordinary move was to "punish" the Russians. The campaign in the Crimea was distinguished by poor planning and incredible blunders by most of the commanding officers, British, French, and Russian alike. The campaign is also famous for great acts of personal courage and endurance.

The French and English troops had landed at Calamita Bay, north of the Russian naval base at Sebastopol, on September 12. They had proceeded south without keeping a supply line open behind them. A vague arrangement was made with the navy to keep pace just off shore. The Russians tried to stop this advance on September 20 at the River Alma, where the first battle was fought. Although the Russians were defeated, it took three days for the allies to pull themselves together and move on.

There were no provisions for carrying the wounded, so the uninjured men gathered them in their arms and lugged them the four or five miles down the river to the coast, where they were picked up by the navy. Since the Russians left all their wounded behind, the allies carried them as well, and the British navy delivered them to Odessa for treatment.

Warfare was a casual business in the nineteenth century. When it was suggested to Lord Raglan that he conceal from the Russians his plan to seize Sebastopol, he replied in shocked tones that such behavior was unbecoming to a British gentleman. He disliked making plans, preferring to view a battle from high ground and direct his troops on the inspiration of the moment. His information about the defenses of Sebastopol was inaccurate, and while

the allies were circling the town, having decided it would
be suicide to try to attack from the north, the Russians
were evacuating because they knew their northern defenses were worthless. The two huge armies missed each
other by a hair.

When the allied plan to attack from the south became
evident, the few Russians left in Sebastopol frantically
began to build up their southern defenses. It took the allies
nearly a month to bring up their big guns and establish a
camp on the Upland. The British used the small harbor of
Balaklava, which was soon overcrowded and filthy. Since
the weather was good they neglected to build a permanent
road up the steep pathway from the town to the British
camp overlooking Sebastopol. It would have been possible
to capture the town and the harbor immediately, but the
French refused to fight. The trouble was that Marshal St.-
Arnaud had died in September, and his inexperienced successor had instructions not to commit the French soldiers
to battle if it could possibly be avoided.

On October 25, the Russians attacked the allies just
before dawn. The little harbor of Balaklava gave its name
to this battle, which was not really a battle but a series of
disconnected engagements. The French kept out of it. The
British won the day but lost the Woronzoff Road, which
had been a great help in moving supplies to the camp. (At
the far end of the road stood the palace belonging to Sidney Herbert's uncle.) Many men were wounded on that
day and were hauled down the dirt path to the harbor,
from where they were shipped to Scutari. Many also died,
the greatest loss being sustained by the Light Brigade. A
confused order had sent the cavalry—in parade-ground

formation, each man a perfect target in his scarlet coat—galloping down a narrow valley with Russian marksmen on each side and cannons firing in their faces.

The Russians attacked the British again on November 5, in a battle similar to Balaklava, this one called for Mount Inkerman. In spite of superior numbers and the usual French refusal to join in, the Russians were again defeated. And once again the dirt path down the hill to Balaklava was witness to the agony of the wounded. Some were strapped to the backs of mules or horses. If they were lucky, a surgeon attended to them once they were on board ship. No provisions had been made for securing the wounded on board and when the sea was stormy they were flung from side to side. The worst suffering was experienced by men who had undergone amputations, which were crudely performed without anesthetics.

There was no harbor at Scutari, so the men were unloaded onto a rickety landing stage. Turkish stretcher-bearers jostled them over the rubbish-strewn ground to the Turkish barracks, now dignified by its new name—the Barrack Hospital.

Florence and her eager party first saw the Barrack Hospital in the pouring rain on the morning of November 4, from the decks of the *Vectis* anchored in the Bosphorus. As the rain cleared, the huge, square building loomed into view from its hilltop, shrouded in misty beauty. Built of yellow brick, it had a tower at each corner. The nursing party was directed to the northwest tower immediately after being rowed ashore on November 5.

The presence of the women sent from England in response to *The Times* criticism of the Army Medical Department was an insult and a threat to all the men who waited to receive Florence Nightingale. However, she was pleasantly surprised by the gracious reception given to her and her party. The officials were all smiles and compliments, but their true feelings were made plain when they withdrew, leaving Florence to squeeze forty-odd people into four small rooms, a kitchen, and a closet. Each room was designed for two people; a similar suite of rooms in another tower was occupied by only one major. Florence separated the nuns and the hospital nurses into three rooms. She put Bracebridge and the interpreter into the fourth room, which was to become her office, and she shared the closet with Mrs. Bracebridge. Mrs. Clark, the invaluable matron from Harley Street who had voluntered to come along and cook for the party, was bedded down in the kitchen.

As the dejected women looked around them, it became perfectly obvious that nothing had been done to make the rooms ready for human occupation. They were damp and filthy, furnished with only a few rickety chairs. There were no beds and no bedding, no food or candles, and there was an abundance of rats and fleas. Some of the nuns found a dead body when they opened the door to their room.

For their first supper Florence managed to obtain some tea, without milk or sugar, and then they lay down on the floor in the dark, trying not to hear the scurrying rats.

The next morning was worse. With icy politeness, the authorities refused Florence's offer of supplies and the services of her nurses. She sought out Macdonald, who was in charge of *The Times* fund, and found that he, too, was being ostracized.

A superficial glance at the wards confirmed her worst suspicions. They lacked the barest necessities. Water was rationed, the food was inadequate, and there was a shortage of bandages and medicines. In the entire place there was not one table on which an operation could be performed. But the army and medical officials insisted that nothing was needed. One false move on Florence's part and they would send her and her nurses packing. In the meantime, no woman was going to perform any service. They were not necessary. The army had always managed without women, and nothing would induce them to change.

In the face of this implacable opposition Florence coolly determined to outwit the army. Her immediate problem, however, was how to control her nurses. They had come all this way to nurse the wounded, they argued, and now Florence forbade them to go into the wards because of some stupid army regulations. She was forcing them to stay in their cramped rooms and sort bandages while men were dying of neglect.

It was at this point that Florence began to demonstrate forcefully her single-mindedness of purpose. Any ordinary woman would have disregarded the authorities and run to help the suffering. But Florence knew that if she did so, she would be expelled by the authorities within a few days. So while men screamed for help, Florence would not allow her nurses to lift a finger without the permission of the army. She believed that if she did not break an army regulation, she would finally win the respect of the authorities and, in the long run, would accomplish her goal.

While outwaiting the authorities, Florence made plans

to assign her nurses. Some were to be used at the General Hospital, a half hour's walk away. She rehearsed the rules of conduct with the women. Nobody was to go out alone under any circumstance. They could walk in threes, or else be escorted by Mrs. Clark. Nobody was to be out after eight o'clock for any reason. Some of the women bitterly resented these rules and came to dislike Florence heartily. Of the original thirty-eight who went with her to Constantinople, she found that six were first-class nurses, sixteen were reliable, and the rest were almost more trouble than they were worth.

Florence did not blame most of the doctors at the Barrack Hospital for the situation. She soon found that the majority were good men trying to do their best under appalling conditions. Her worst enemies were the officers who would not depart from army regulations, even when the regulations were obviously wrong, and even when they had written instructions from Sidney Herbert to waive the rules in order to save lives.

Florence had the utmost respect for regulations and obeyed most of them to the letter. She always knew exactly what she was doing, and on the infrequent occasion when she would sweep all rules aside and accomplish a minor miracle, it was invariably applauded by the authorities in London. As the doctors caustically remarked, she had been invited to dinner by more than half the Cabinet and had powerful connections with the ruling families of England. She also had money. She and Macdonald between them had more than thirty thousand pounds to spend as they thought fit, and Florence also had her personal fortune to spend. She was as generous and careless about money as her mother was, and bought whatever the soldiers needed without counting the cost.

The people in charge of both the Barrack Hospital and the arrangements for supplying the army and the hospitals were not bold men. When things got out of hand they simply did not know what to do. After forty years of peace, the method of supplying and transporting the army had fallen into confusion from lack of practice. The inept men in charge were moved to Scutari and told to produce horses and supplies quickly. They simply did not know how. Furthermore, nobody was clear about the division of responsibility. There were two departments in charge of supplying the army—the Commissariat and the Purveyor's Department. A man named Filder was the Commissary General, and he had three inexperienced clerks to help him organize transportation, food, and all necessary supplies for the original army of twenty-five thousand men. He was required to place the bulk of his orders with English merchants, which was sensible enough in peacetime. However, in wartime it was ridiculous to wait for emergency supplies to come from England when Contantinople, one of the world's greatest markets, was only a short boat ride away.

The purveyor was a seventy-year-old man named Ward, who was clear about one thing—he did not have the authority to purchase anything. His duties included providing special diets for men in poor health, but he could not issue them without permission from Filder. Enormous numbers of forms passed back and forth between the two departments. Everything had to be signed and countersigned and duplicated, and both men were punctilious in this matter. To add to the confusion, both departments were governed by warrants. These were lists of what each department might issue, and neither man dared to issue anything not on his warrant.

The chaos resulting from this setup was unbelievable. Men died for want of supplies that were in the stores across the Bosphorus. Men who could not eat the regular hospital food also died of starvation. A doctor would issue a form to Ward requesting a special food. Ward would order it from Filder. If Filder was too busy or did not have the specific food, he would write "none in store" on the form and that was the end of that. The doctor was powerless to see that his orders were carried out.

Winter blankets and clothing were not issued to the freezing, half-naked men because these items were not listed on the warrants of either Filder or Ward. Other supplies were not issued because the officers responsible had not inspected them and signed them out, or they were packed so deep in the holds of the ships carrying arms that they sailed on through to the Crimea and were never seen again.

The neglect of the common soldier was accepted by the army as inevitable. What was new was the on-the-spot reporting of the brutal sufferings sustained by soldiers and aggravated unnecessarily by poor management.

The outcry that resulted from exposing these conditions in *The Times* had brought about not only Florence's appointment, but also Parliament's decision to send commissioners to inquire into the treatment of the sick. The first commissioners arrived in Constantinople at the same time that Florence did.

Some of the commissioners were sent at the request of a Mr. Roebuck, the member of Parliament for Sheffield. He was the chairman of a special parliamentary committee called the Roebuck Committee, which received the commissioners' report and conducted a full-scale inquiry into the conduct of the war and the care of the wounded. But Florence wanted commissioners with power to act on the spot. She wrote to her old friend Lord Ashley, telling him exactly what was needed. He responded with a three-man sanitary commission with full executive powers. These commissioners had the authority of Parliament to override the Army Medical Department, and to carry out changes in the hospitals suggested by Florence.

CHAPTER

✴✴✴✴✴✴✴✴✴
VI
✴✴✴✴✴✴✴✴✴

The Barrack Hospital, Scutari

The commissioners concentrated their investigations on the Barrack Hospital in Scutari. Conditions at the General Hospital were not nearly as serious, since that building was actually designed to be a hospital and had a reasonably sound construction. The commissioners found that the Barrack Hospital was a pesthouse. When the army had used the building as its headquarters, horses had been stabled there. The inner courtyard had been used as a garbage dump and had never been cleaned out. Temporary latrines had been dug in the courtyard, which also fouled the atmosphere.

When Florence and her party arrived, every drain in the building was stopped up. The flushing systems of the indoor toilets did not work, and the overflow was ankle-deep in the adjoining rooms.

Augustus Stafford, a member of Parliament on a private

visit to Scutari, asked Dr. Menzies, the Chief Army Medical Officer, to have the lavatories cleaned. The doctor said that he was not responsible. Stafford then asked Major Sillery, Military Commandant of the hospital, who replied that he did not know where the money would come from, and he did not have instructions about the lavatories anyway. Stafford offered to pay for the cleaning out of his own pocket, but the outraged major refused. The lavatories remained dirty.

The patients who could walk refused to go near the lavatories. (There were no warrants for issuing them robes or slippers.) So the army finally set up huge tubs as urinals at the ends of the wards. The ward orderlies were responsible for emptying the tubs, and persistently neglected their duty. Florence asked that the tubs be emptied. Her technique was to stand in silence beside a tub and wait until her order was obeyed. Sometimes she had to stand for more than an hour, but the tubs were finally emptied. Florence counted twenty chamber pots when there were more than one thousand men in the hospital suffering from acute diarrhea.

When the commissioners began the cleaning-up process, they had the drainage system traced. It ended in a series of open cesspools under the building, all of which were overflowing.

What made matters worse was the material construction of the building. The walls were of porous plaster which absorbed moisture from the cesspools, and the contamination was carried throughout the building. Men who were put in certain beds always died no matter how slight their injuries or sicknesses. Those beds were the ones nearest to the lavatories where the odors were the worst and the atmosphere surrounding them was as lethal as poison gas.

The Barrack Hospital was chronically short of water. Because of the nature of many of the diseases, the commissioners ordered that the drinking-water system be traced. It was a bitter moment when the diggers uncovered the body of a dead horse adding to the contamination that the commissioners had already suspected.

After four months, some of the commissioners made their report to the Roebuck Committee. Roebuck had used some of their information to topple the government. A vote of no confidence, in January, 1855, had forced the Cabinet to resign. Although the Army Medical Department was trying to get rid of her, Florence's position was not threatened by the new government because the prime minister was now her old friend Lord Palmerston. With the exchange of governments, Sidney Herbert gave up his position, but continued to receive reports from Florence and to exercise his influence behind the scenes.

Florence had guessed most of the problems before the commissioners uncovered them. But these were things that she was powerless to remedy, and it took the direct intervention of Lord Ashley's Sanitary Commission to set them straight. Florence's strategy was to obey the doctors, win their confidence, and then seize every opportunity to work for the good of the patients. While her nurses chafed and grumbled she looked for an opening. A natural job for the women was cooking hot cereals and other bland foods for the men who were too ill to digest meat.

Some of the patients in the hospital actually died of starvation. Meals were never served on time, and were of

Florence Nightingale — the Lady with the Lamp
(All photos courtesy The Bettmann Archive)

Florence Nightingale's home.

Supervising the hospital at Scutari

Florence Nightingale's carriage during the Crimean War

At Scutari, 1854

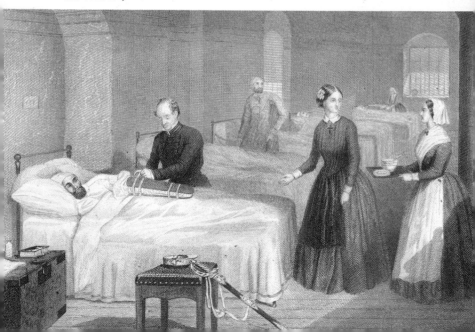

Florence Nightingale, 1873

such inferior quality that they could not always be eaten. The one kitchen was equipped with thirteen huge cooking pots suspended over wood fires. In keeping with the other shortages was the lack of dry wood. The cooks had to use green wood which smoked and smoldered, and sometimes the water in the pots did not boil. It was the job of the ward orderlies to serve the meals. They collected the ration of meat for their ward, tied it up, dumped it in the cooking pots, and collected it again when the cook said it was ready. The orderlies divided the meat and distributed it. Some portions were all gristle or bone, the food was always cold, and sometimes it was half raw as well. Tea was made in the same pots, which were not washed because of the water shortage.

The day that Florence first offered her services—Sunday, November 6—was the day that the first of the wounded from the Battle of Balaklava began to arrive. Although the official policy was to pretend that she did not exist, a few of the doctors asked her to cook some hot arrowroot, a nourishing starch rather like cornstarch in appearance, and to warm some port wine. She complied only when she received a request written on the correct form and signed by a doctor. She countersigned the form and the food was taken to the man in need. Soon other requests followed. The Army Medical Department seemed to feel that its pride could not be further damaged by a woman cooking delicacies. It was a perfect way for Florence to get some of her nurses into the wards, although she forbade them to touch a patient or to help in any other way.

There was, of course, no kitchen for cooking special diets. The few supplies that existed were cooked by the

orderlies over small fires right in the wards. All through
the winter Florence herself supplied most of the food
for special diets. She set up the portable cooking stoves
from Marseilles in the tiny kitchen in her northwest tower,
and she used the food that she had brought with her.
When these supplies were exhausted she bought more in
Constantinople. Before many weeks had passed, the hospital authorities found themselves relying on Florence to
save the men with intestinal sicknesses from starvation.
This contribution alone vindicated her presence in Scutari.

Dr. Menzies did not feel offended by the sight of
women on their hands and knees, so when Florence ap-
proached him for permission to scrub the floors he granted
it readily. Cleaning was women's work, and the ward orderlies had refused to clean the wards anyway. Florence
asked Macdonald to take the next boat over to Constantinople and buy scrubbing brushes and sacking with money
from *The Times* fund. In his evidence before the Roebuck Committee, Macdonald would report: "The first improvements took place after Miss Nightingale's arrival—
greater cleanliness and greater order. I recollect one of the
first things she asked me to supply was 200 hard scrubbers
and sacking for washing the floors, for which no means
existed at that time."

Not surprisingly, the Barrack Hospital was infested
with vermin. The commissioners ordered the disinfecting
of the walls and had whitewash applied throughout the
building. Florence decided to do something about the
men's clothes and bedding, where it existed. The Army
Medical Department had not managed any satisfactory arrangement for washing. Clothes sent to the laundry, which

was operated by a nonmilitary man, came back with more vermin than when they had been sent. Again permission was granted for the women to take over this menial task. Dr. Menzies even agreed that some men from the Engineers Corps could install boilers in a house that Florence rented near the hospital, with money from *The Times* fund. Work at the washhouse was soon in full swing, and the vermin problem was slowly reduced by boiling every sheet and article of clothing.

Florence's nurses were not the only women in Scutari. Some of the soldiers had their wives with them and Florence enlisted them to help with the wash. Most of them were glad to earn some money, and their services would free the nurses for medical duties if the time ever came.

The camp prostitutes were another matter, but Florence did her best for them, too. She put them in the care of Lady Alicia Blackwood, a volunteer who had come from England with her husband, the Reverend Dr. Blackwood, who became a military chaplain. Lady Alicia offered to help in any way that she could, and she recorded the following conversation with Florence.

"Do you mean what you say?" asked Florence.

"Yes, certainly; why do you ask me?"

"Because I have had several such applications before, and when I have suggested work, I found it could not be done, or some excuse was made; it was not exactly the sort of thing intended, it required special suitability, &."

"Well," I replied, "I am in earnest; we came out here with no other wish than to help where we could."

"Very well, then, you really can help me if you

will. In this Barrack are now located some two hundred poor women in the most abject misery . . . they
are in rags and covered with vermin. My heart bleeds
for them; but my work is with the soldiers. . . .
Now will you undertake to look after them? If you
will take them as your charge, I will send an orderly
who will show you their haunts."

Lady Alicia accepted the assignment and took the
women under her care. She established a maternity hospital, and fed and clothed the children as well. The
women who were cooperative were employed sorting linen
and making bandages.

While the Army Medical Department steadfastly refused the services of nurses in the wards, and the most that
Florence could hope to achieve was "greater cleanliness
and greater order," there was a dramatic change in the
conduct of the war in the Crimea.

It was simply that winter had arrived, and the army was
not prepared for it. Winter was a far more serious enemy
than the Russians, and claimed more victims than all the
battles of the war put together. After the Battle of Inkerman there was no more fighting until the spring. The allies
settled to the south of Sebastopol and considered that they
were besieging the town. However, they neglected to sur-
round it, and Russian troops and supplies entered without
interference.

Many men were already sick when, on November 14,
1854, the Crimea was swept by a terrible hurricane. Tents
and supplies were blown away and the wretched army was
left to face the bitter winter weather without the barest

necessities of life. That evening, snow began to fall. It
blanketed the Upland, destroyed the dirt path down to the
harbor of Balaklava, and rested on the wreckage of the
fleet destroyed at anchor by the wind. By the end of that
month, eight thousand men were in the hospitals.

The condition of the soldiers who had made the journey
across the Black Sea was pitiful beyond belief. At the landing stage at Scutari, the careless stretcher-bearers picked up
men with battle wounds, as well as those suffering from
dysentery, typhoid, cholera, frostbite, exposure, and starvation. It was a catastrophe that continued all through the
winter. The Barrack Hospital was deluged by the sick, and
the torrent reached its worst proportions in December and
January. Men lay for two weeks in the same clothes in
which they arrived, without seeing a doctor. In the general
panic, Dr. Menzies commanded every able-bodied person
—including the nurses—to help feed and wash the men
and cover their open wounds until a doctor could attend
to them.

Florence organized the nurses to make palliasses out of
sacking and straw, since the hospital had run out of beds.
The new patients were set on these all along the corridors
and hallways, in every available space. On the day of the
hurricane Florence wrote to one of her doctor friends in
Harley Street:

We have had such a Sea in the Bosphorus, and the
Turks, the very men for whom we are fighting, carry
in our Wounded so cruelly, that they arrive in a state
of Agony. One amputated Stump died 2 hours after
we received him, one compound Fracture just as we

were getting him into Bed—in all, twenty-four cases died on the day of landing. The Dysentery Cases have died at the rate of one in two. . . . We have now four miles of Beds and not eighteen inches apart. . . . The wounded are now lying up to our very door, and we are landing 540 more from the "Andes." Every ten minutes an Orderly runs, and we have to go and cram lint into the wound till a Surgeon can be sent for, and stop the Bleeding as well as we can.

Under these conditions, the medical authorities had no time to worry about their fear of Miss Nightingale. It did not take long for the frantic doctors to realize that when something was needed and the supply departments failed them, all they had to do was to ask Florence. She had managed to find out what actually was stored in the storerooms. She made up daily lists of what was needed and sent the invaluable Macdonald to Constantinople to buy supplies. In this way, she simply took over the work that Filder and Ward failed to do, and became the actual purveyor of both the Barrack and General hospitals.

In one of her letters to Sidney Herbert, Florence wrote with characteristic good humor: "I am a kind of General Dealer, in socks, shirts, knives and forks, wooden spoons, tin baths, tables and forms, cabbages and carrots, operating tables, towels and soap, small tooth combs, precipitate for destroying lice, scissors, bedpans and stump pillows."

A description of the kitchen in Florence's headquarters in the "Sisters' Tower," as the northwest tower soon came to be called, was written by one of the lady volunteers.

From this room were distributed quantities of arrowroot, sago, rice puddings, jelly, beef tea, and lemonade upon requisition made by the surgeons. This caused great comings to and fro; numbers of orderlies were waiting at the door with requisitions. One of the nuns or a lady received them, and saw they were signed and countersigned before serving. We used, among ourselves, to call this kitchen the tower of Babel. In the middle of the day everything and everybody seemed to be there; boxes, parcels, bundles of sheets, shirts, and old linen and flannels, tubs of butter, sugar, bread, kettles, saucepans, heaps of books, and of all kinds of rubbish besides the diets which were being dispensed; then the people, ladies, nuns, nurses, orderlies, Turks, Greeks, French and Italian servants, officers and others waiting to see Miss Nightingale; all pacing to and fro, all intent upon their own business and all speaking their own language.

Every spare minute of the day and late into the night, Florence was writing. She wrote letters, reports, lists, accounts, and suggestions for the reorganization of the Army Medical Department and other sections of the army besides. How she ever found time to be a nurse as well is an unanswered question. She was raised in luxury, accustomed to the finest food, a comfortable bed, and servants to wait on her. Yet in Scutari she lived under conditions of privation, constantly without proper food or sleep, and exposed to foul diseases. Despite it, she was the best nurse in the entire hospital. By concentrating on tasks that the doctors looked on as natural for women, she won their confidence, and they were soon glad to have the nurses perform medical duties. Nobody knows just exactly when the change occurred. But one thing is certain; the acceptance of women by the British army was due entirely to the way in which Florence handled a difficult situation.

Florence the nurse was a far different woman from Florence the organizer. Her gentleness and skill were unequaled. She would spend hours on her knees dressing wounds. When a shipload of wounded arrived she often did not get to bed at all. On one occasion five men were abandoned to die, and Florence asked permission to take care of them. She tended them herself, dressed their wounds, fed and washed them. The next morning the doctors found them in good enough condition to be operated on. She invariably nursed the worst cases herself, and was present at as many operations as was possible, to strengthen the patient by her presence. She never let a man die alone, and only very occasionally would she allow Mrs. Bracebridge to take her place. Even when a man had lost consciousness Florence would remain on her knees, holding his hand until the end.

One of the most astonishing things was that amid all the horror, Florence remained cheerful. Some of the survivors described how she could laugh and joke with the men, and cheer them when they were downhearted. She had an amazing effect on them. They called her a blessed angel from heaven, and would not swear or be caught drinking when she was present.

Perhaps the most famous description of Florence at Scutari was written by Macdonald. Every night she used to make a final round of the wards, and tend to those who needed help. Macdonald wrote:

She is a "ministering angel" without any exaggeration in these hospitals, and as her slender form glides quietly along each corridor, every poor fellow's face softens with gratitude at the sight of her. When all the medical officers have retired for the night and silence and darkness have settled down upon those miles of prostrate sick, she may be observed alone, with a little lamp in her hand, making her solitary rounds.

The Side of the Angels

Florence had gone to Scutari with one aim in mind, to make nursing a dignified profession by demonstrating that women could work with the Army Medical Department. But while she was there she added another cause to her life, the improvement of the lot of the common soldier.

In January, 1855, there were twelve thousand men in hospitals, almost half the original army that had been sent to the Crimea. It has been roughly estimated that three quarters of the deaths in the hospitals were due to diseases and not to battle wounds. With proper planning and sanitary conditions, thousands of lives could have been saved. Florence was haunted by the faces of those men whose lives had been so cruelly squandered. When she returned home she said, "I stand at the altar of the murdered men, and while I live I will fight their cause."

One soldier wrote: "What a comfort it was to see her

pass even. She would speak to one, and nod and smile to many more; but she could not do it all you know. We lay there by hundreds; but we could kiss her shadow as it fell and lay our heads on the pillow again content."

One of Florence's nurses wrote: "I much admired her manner to the men—it was so tender and kind."

The men's response to her was one of the few consolations that Florence enjoyed. She said: "Never came from any of them one word nor one look which a gentleman would not have used; and while paying this humble tribute to humble courtesy, the tears come into my eyes as I think how, amid scenes of loathsome disease and death, there arose above it all the innate dignity, gentleness and chivalry of the men . . . shining in the midst of what must be considered the lowest sinks of human misery, and preventing instinctively the use of one expression which could distress a gentlewoman."

Florence had expected help from the British Ambassador to Constantinople. She knew that Sidney Herbert had written to him, instructing him to spend whatever money was needed to remedy the deplorable situation in the hospitals. Lord Stratford had, indeed, asked Dr. Menzies what he needed. When the official reply of "nothing is lacking" came back, Lord Stratford accepted it. He never visited the Barrack or the General Hospital, and remained indifferent to the plight of the common soldiers, who were suffering and dying within sight of the palace where he lived.

Lord Stratford was at the height of a brilliant diplomatic career, and a pet idea of his was to build a Protestant chapel in Constantinople. Since the hospitals had "all they needed," he wanted to use The Times fund to put up his

chapel. Florence had no use for this great nobleman, and
her remarks about him were spiked with venom. There is
no record of any conversation between them, although
Florence did attend a reception at the British Embassy on
Christmas Day, 1855. When Florence had arrived in Scutari, Lord Stratford had sent one of his aides to meet her,
and all other negotiations were handled by Lady Stratford.

Almost immediately Florence appealed to Lady Stratford for help But Lady Stratford refused to come over; she
said that on her only visit to Scutari the smell had made
her sick. However, she did offer to get something for
Florence in Constantinople, so Florence asked for twelve
heavy wagons to help carry the wounded up from the landing stage to the hospital. For a joke, Lady Stratford sent
seven glass coaches and five other unsuitable carriages.
Without a word, Florence paid them off out of her own
pocket.

About a month later, Florence, in desperation, appealed
to Lady Stratford again. One side of the Barrack Hospital
had burned down and there was no money to rebuild it.
The overcrowding had reached fantastic proportions, and
Florence was determined to get the wing ready for an
expected shipment of sick men.

Lady Stratford was persuaded to come to Scutari and
discuss the rebuilding proposal. She refused to enter the
hospital, but finally agreed that 125 Turkish workmen
should be employed to do the job. They struck for higher
wages almost immediately. Florence now wrote to Lord
Stratford entreating him to help. He ignored her, so she
took matters into her own hands. Out of her own money

she hired 200 workmen and goaded them into finishing the work on time. She procured all the necessary furnishings, and in a triumph of efficiency greeted every sick man with food and water. Everybody was washed and given clean clothes, every wound was dressed, and every man was put into a clean bed. One soldier remarked: "We thought we were in heaven."

This one incident, perhaps more than any other, had made the top officials of the Army Medical Department declare total war against Florence. While a whispering campaign was started against her reputation, and the insolent younger medical officers called her "the Bird" behind her back, Florence was pouring out her ideas on paper. The contempt with which she described some of these officers is startling.

She wrote to Sidney Herbert: "In a time of such calamity, unparalleled in the history, I believe, of calamity, I have a little compassion left even for the wretched Purveyor, swamped amid demands he never expected. But I have no compassion for the men who would rather see hundreds of lives lost than waive one scruple of the official conscience."

Florence proposed absolute cleanliness in all military hospitals and barracks. She advocated army medical schools for the further training of doctors, and many revolutionary ideas concerning the keeping of records and statistics. Postmortems, she said, should be held to determine precisely the causes of death. She had a good grasp of logistics as they concerned keeping the hospitals supplied. She was shrewd enough to guess that many of the supplies that Sidney Herbert had said were sent were actually in

the Turkish customhouses, tangled up in regulations.
She drew up lists of the numbers of officers that were really
needed and she described their duties. She proposed
proper training for a permanent body of orderlies. These
are her ideas about serving meals:

> Let a Commissariat Officer reside here—let the Ward-
> Masters make a total from the Diet Rolls of the
> Medical Men—so many hundred full diets—so many
> hundred half diets—so many hundred spoon diets,
> and give it over to the Commissariat Officer the day
> before. The next day the whole quantity, the total of
> all the Ward-Masters' totals, is given into the kitch-
> ens direct.
>
> It should be all carved in the kitchens on hot
> plates, and at meal-times the Orderlies come to fetch
> it for the patients—carry it through the wards, where
> an Officer takes it off to every bed, according to the
> Bed-ticket, on which he reads the Diet hung up at
> every bed. The time and confusion thus saved would
> be incalculable. Punctuality is now impossible; the
> food is half raw, and often many hours after time.
> Some of the portions are all bone, whereas the meat
> should be boned in the kitchen, according to the plan
> now proposed, and the portions there carved contain
> meat only. Pray consider this.

Few of these dreams were actually realized at Scutari,
but Florence's ideas were so practical that many of them
were eventually adopted. However, she did enjoy one
triumph at the Barrack Hospital—the reorganization of the
kitchen. Alexis Soyer, the chef at the Reform Club, one of

London's fanciest, was so moved by the stories about the war that he went to Scutari in March, 1855, at his own expense, and volunteered to cook for the troops. He and Florence worked together, and the food improved in a dramatic fashion. They lost their fight for permission to bone the meat in the kitchen, but Soyer was an artist at making poor-quality meat taste good. His soups were tasty and nourishing, and the tantalizing aroma of freshly baked bread and biscuits revived everybody's flagging spirits.

Queen Victoria expressed a desire to see the reports sent by Miss Nightingale. In a letter to Sidney Herbert, the Queen wrote: "Let Mrs. Herbert also know that I wish Miss Nightingale and the ladies would tell these poor noble wounded and sick men that no-one takes a warmer interest or feels more for their sufferings or admires their courage and heroism more than their Queen."

Made bold by this expression of sympathy, Florence wrote directly to the Queen, asking two favors. Every wounded man lost 4 ½d a day out of his pay, and every sick man lost 9d. Florence asked that every man whose sickness was due to being on active service in the presence of the enemy lose only 4 ½d. The Queen acted immediately, and the men's pay at the new rate was made retroactive to the Battle of the River Alma. Florence also asked that the military cemeteries at Scutari be turned over to the British, and the Queen arranged that, too.

Thousands of letters poured in to Florence, thanking her for her kindness to the soldiers. Many requested news about sons or fathers, and had messages for them. Florence wrote thousands of replies. The following is one example:

. . . The first time I saw your son was in going

round the wards in the General Hospital at Balaklava. He had been brought in, in the morning. . . .
He was always conscious, and remained so till the
very last. He prayed aloud so beautifully that, as the
Nurse in charge said, "It was like a sermon to hear
him." He asked "to see Miss Nightingale." He knew
me, and expressed himself to me as entirely resigned
to die. He pressed my hand when he could not speak.
He died in the night. . . . He was decently interred
in a burial-ground we have about a mile from Balaklava. One of my own Sisters lies in the same ground,
to whom I have erected a monument. Should you
wish anything similar to be done over the grave of
your lost son, I will endeavour to gratify you, if you
will inform me of your wishes. With true sympathy
for your loss, I remain, dear Madam, yours sincerely,
Florence Nightingale.

Florence had revolutionary ideas, too, for the conva-
lescent men. In May, 1855, she opened a small reading
room at Scutari. So many men flocked there that she tried
to get a teacher to instruct the illiterate, but she was defeated by the military authorities. She was told that the
men were only interested in drink. However, she fought
for permission to close the drink shops of Scutari and to
have the streets patrolled at night, and she won those
fights.

In September, Florence opened the Inkerman Coffee
House with a recreation room. She furnished it with her
own money and provided writing materials, books, and
maps. There was so much interest in the project that by the
spring of 1856 she had opened four schools for the soldiers,

with professional teachers, and had organized a choir; an amateur theatrical group; games of dominoes and chess; football games and other outdoor sports.

Florence made many contacts with soldiers' families, and was sympathetic to their poverty. Another of her ideas was that the men should send money home rather than squander it on drink, but she found that none of the soldiers believed that their families would ever receive money sent via the army system. So she simply collected the money and asked Bracebridge or Macdonald to buy regular postal orders. In a short time more than £1,000 was sent home to grateful families.

When some of the soldiers returned to active duty, they asked if they might continue to send money home by buying postal orders. The request was refused. Florence wrote to Queen Victoria. The Queen sent the letter to Lord Palmerston, with a request that he promote Miss Nightingale's idea. Palmerston got Cabinet approval, the army was overruled, and post offices were opened in Scutari, Constantinople, Balaklava, and the camp outside Sebastopol. In less than six months, £71,000 in postal orders was sent home.

Before Florence was through, the army was so shaken up that things could never return to the way they were before the Crimean War. She won for the common soldier the right to be considered a human being. She initiated the army recreational program, and after she returned home, she continued to needle the authorities to overhaul all the army barracks and hospital facilities.

CHAPTER

✼✼✼✼✼✼✼✼✼
VIII
✼✼✼✼✼✼✼✼✼

The Side of the Devils

Although Florence accomplished amazing things during her stay in the East, her relationships with some of her nurses and with the Army Medical Department in general continually tottered on the brink of disaster. She was overwhelmed by the difficulties of these relationships, and often obsessed by a sense of failure. The strain of constant death and disaster affected everyone who was trying to work under these appalling circumstances. One case was the scandal of Sister Elizabeth Wheeler.

Sister Elizabeth was a simple, devoted woman who found the whole complicated mess of army politics too much for her. She had volunteered to nurse soldiers, and she refused to understand the restraints that Florence put on the nursing expedition. Her main job was to distribute food from the diet kitchen. To relieve her feelings, she wrote passionate letters home accusing Florence of deliberately starving the men. One letter was published in *The Times* on December 8, 1854, and it provoked a storm. In it, Sister Elizabeth described the doctors as brutal and indifferent to suffering. The Hospitals Commission held an inquiry and established the gross inaccuracy of some of Sister Elizabeth's statements.

The nun was asked to resign, and was sent home. Even though the commission's verdict favored Florence; the incident did her a lot of harm. It showed that she did not control all her nurses, and the adverse publicity worsened her relations with the Army Medical Department.

The case of Mary Stanley dealt a blow to Florence's authority from which she never really recovered. Mary Stanley had met Florence in Rome sometime before, and the two young women had struck up a friendship. Both became good friends of the Herberts, and both were interested in nursing and hospital reform. Mary had helped Florence to choose the original party for Scutari, and now she yearned to show the world that she could do just as well as Florence, and perhaps better.

Mary asked permission from Sidney Herbert to go to Constantinople with another party of nurses to help Florence. It sounded like an eminently sensible idea. Understaffing was one of Florence's problems, and it never occurred to Herbert that she would be anything but pleased with extra hands to lighten the load. He did not yet understand that Florence was having a terrible time trying to control her own nurses, let alone the forty-six more that Mary brought along. Florence had originally wanted only a very small group, and she had been persuaded to enlarge the party against her better judgment. The news of Mary's arrival was made known on December 14, 1854; Mary and her nurses arrived on the fifteenth.

Florence wrote Sidney a blistering letter tendering her resignation. When she finally realized that he was innocent in the matter, they were reconciled, but her friendship with Mary was definitely ended.

Mary had brought many nuns with her, including a group which had their own mother superior, Mother Bridgeman. This was a flagrant violation of Florence's orders that each nun or nurse had to obey her and no one else. Besides, England in the nineteenth century was vigorously anti-Catholic, and there had already been criticism concerning the number of nuns working with the soldiers. Mary was secretly received into the Roman Catholic Church while in Constantinople, and she brought some nuns with her solely for the purpose of converting soldiers to the Roman Catholic Church. She also brought the English class distinctions with her, again in direct opposition to Florence. According to Mary, there were ladies who spoke kindly to the men, and there were maids who did the dirty work.

When Mary arrived, she was refused permission to land for the simple reason that there was no place in any of the hospitals for her and her party. They had spent all their money on the journey, and Florence, when she cooled down, came to their rescue with a considerable sum of money.

A house was found for them that belonged to the British Embassy, and the new group became the center of a bitter Roman Catholic–Protestant controversy. Eventually, some of the second party were accepted at the Barrack Hospital, some at the General Hospital, and Florence sent some of her party home to England to make room for them.

A group under Elizabeth Davis, a woman whom Florence did not trust, escaped Florence's jurisdiction by going to Balaklava where there was another general hospital. Mary, determined to have her own way, opened her own hospital in an empty Turkish barracks at Koulali on the Bosphorus.

Mary Stanley's hospital was opened without the permission of the Army Medical Department. She took Mother Bridgeman and her nuns to help her, and the hospital was run on the "lady" plan. The story makes pitiful reading. Wounded men descended upon them when nothing was ready. The ladies refused to get their hands dirty despite the desperate situation, and an appalling number of men died from neglect. Mary became hysterical and could not control the hospital. It remained filthy and verminous, stores were stolen, the Army Medical Department refused to send help, and Mary went home to England.

The hospital at Koulali collapsed, and Mother Bridgeman, without Florence's knowledge, took her nuns to the Crimea. There she allied herself with Florence's enemy, Dr. John Hall, the officer in charge of all the Army Medical Department on active duty. Hall made Mother Bridgeman the superintendent of the General Hospital in Balaklava, ignoring Florence's authority over all the nurses in the area. Although Florence maintained cordial personal relations with Mother Bridgeman, she never succeeded in bringing her under control.

Mary Stanley contributed another unfortunate legacy. Many people in England, including Queen Victoria, sent gifts to the troops. They were known as "free gifts," and Florence kept account of them and how they were used. The burden of accounting and correspondence was so great that she finally delegated the responsibility to Mrs. Bracebridge. When the Bracebridges returned to England, Florence hired a Miss Salisbury to do the work. Miss Salisbury stole from the "free gifts" store, and when her theft was discovered, she begged for mercy. In order to avoid a scandal, Florence sent the woman home to England, where Miss Salisbury promptly accused Florence of stealing and was received with open arms by Mary Stanley. Together they drew up a formal complaint against Florence and presented it to the War Office. Dr. Hall's friends in the War Office chose to make a serious case out of the complaint, and they demanded an official inquiry.

The arduous winter had left Florence in very weak physical condition. As spring came to the Crimea, the number of the sick decreased and conditions became somewhat better in the various hospitals. This improvement gave Florence's enemies more time to consider how to harass her.

In March, 1855, Dr. Hall appointed a Dr. Lawson to be in charge of the Barrack Hospital. Dr. Lawson had been the villain of the *Avon* scandal. Wounded men had been loaded onto the *Avon* and abandoned for two weeks, with only one assistant surgeon to tend to several hundreds of them. Lord Raglan held an inquiry which censured Dr. Lawson and pinned part of the blame on Dr. Hall. Lord Raglan recommended that Dr. Lawson be dismissed, but Dr. Hall asserted his authority by promoting Lawson to Scutari. This appointment was greeted with dismay, and many of Florence's staunchest allies among the doctors were afraid to cooperate with her anymore.

By May, 1855, Florence felt that things were really under control in Scutari, as far as the patients in the two hospitals were concerned, so she decided to go to the Crimea itself. Dr. Hall was in charge of the General Hospital at Balaklava, his purveyor was a David Fitz-Gerald, and the kitchen was supervised by Elizabeth Davis.

On May 5, Florence sailed into the harbor at Balaklava. She was greeted enthusiastically by the troops and by the army officers, but when she went to inspect the hospital she was told that she had no authority there.

Wearily, Florence climbed up to a collection of huts, called the Castle Hospital, where the overflow of wounded was accommodated. At the end of the day she collapsed. She became delirious and her life was in danger for nearly three weeks. After a cursory examination by Dr. Hadley, a friend of Dr. Hall's, she was nursed by Mrs. Roberts, who was Florence's best nurse. As skillful in dressing wounds as some of the surgeons, Mrs. Roberts could neither read nor write. Mrs. Bracebridge came as quickly as she could, and when Florence could be moved it was decided to take her to a private house in Scutari.

Dr. Hall and Dr. Hadley booked passage for Florence on board the *Jura*. Just before sailing time, Bracebridge discovered that the ship was bound directly for England, without a stop at Scutari. They all hurried off and were taken to Scutari by a friend on his steam yacht. The discovery of the trick that the doctors had tried to play on her did not help Florence's recovery, and it was July before she was strong enough to return to the Barrack Hospital.

During Florence's illness things had changed for the worse, but she was determined to go back to Balaklava and fight it out with Dr. Hall. In the meantime her authority was completely disregarded in the Crimea. Lord Raglan, who had always supported Florence, had died. His replacement, General Simpson, was opposed to nursing and had not received clear instructions from London about Florence's position. The Bracebridges decided to go home, and Florence was miserable without them. When she was able to work again, she found much hostility from the doctors, who feared reprisals from Dr. Hall if they were found cooperating with "the Bird."

Aunt Mai came to the rescue, and arrived at Scutari on September 18, 1855. When she first caught sight of Florence she burst into tears. Thin and pale, Florence had had all her hair cut off when she was ill and the fine baby curls made her look pathetic. Aunt Mai could not believe the volume of work that Florence undertook each day, and she was amazed at the insolence handed out to her niece. Mai was able to relieve Florence of some of the paper work, but she could not stop her from going back to the Crimea in October.

The war had dragged on. Finally, on September 8, 1855, the British and French allies captured the ruins that had once been the city of Sebastopol. When Florence arrived in the Crimea, peace feelers had already been extended by both sides. At first she maintained polite relationships with Dr. Hall, Fitz-Gerald, and Mother Bridgeman, but all her careful work was destroyed once and for all when a copy of *The Times*, dated October 16, 1855, was sent to Balaklava.

Bracebridge had made a speech at the town hall in

Coventry. He launched an all-out attack on the Army
Medical Department, which was naturally interpreted as
an accurate portrayal of Florence's feelings, too. The
speech played right into Dr. Hall's hands.

Hall wrote to his superior in London:

> When one reads such twaddling nonsense as that
> uttered by Mr. Bracebridge and which was so much
> lauded in *The Times* because the garrulous old gen-
> tleman talked about Miss Nightingale putting hospi-
> tals containing three or four thousand patients in
> order in a couple of days by means of *The Times'*
> fund, one cannot suppress a feeling of contempt for
> the ignorant multitude who are deluded by these
> fairy tales.

Florence was powerless to undo the damage. On November 5, she wrote to Aunt Mai at Scutari: "I have been
appointed a twelvemonth today, and what a twelvemonth
of dirt it has been, of experience which would sadden not
a life but eternity. Who has ever had a sadder experience.
Christ was betrayed by one, but my cause has been betrayed by everyone. . . . Dr. Hall is dead against me. He
descends to every meanness to make my position more
difficult."

By the end of the month she had succeeded in building
an extra diet kitchen, when a cholera epidemic sent her
sailing back to Scutari. Miraculously, Florence survived
another bitter winter. Only Aunt Mai knew how ill she
really was. One of the guests at the Embassy Christmas
party on Christmas Day, 1855, wrote the following description:

> By the side of the Ambassadress was a tall, fashion-

able, haughty beauty. But the next instant my eye wandered to a lady modestly standing on the other side of Lady Stratford. . . . Yes, it was Florence Nightingale, greatest of all now in name and honour among women. I assure you that I was glad not to be obliged to speak just then, for I felt quite dumb as I looked at her wasted figure and the short brown hair combed over her forehead like a child's, cut so when her life was despaired of from a fever but a short time ago.

Her dress . . . was black, made high to the throat, its only ornament being a large enamelled brooch. . . . Only her plain black dress, quiet manner and great renown told so powerfully altogether in that assembly of brilliant dress and uniforms. She is very slight, rather above the middle height; her face is long and thin, but this may be from recent illness and great fatigue. She has a very prominent nose, slightly Roman; and small dark eyes, kind, yet penetrating; but her face does not give you at all the idea of great talent. . . . She was still very weak, and could not join in the games, but she sat on a sofa, and looked on, laughing until the tears came into her eyes.

The brooch was a gift from Queen Victoria, who expressed the hope that Florence would come to see her on her return home. There were only a few agonizing months left, and Florence was determined to stay to the bitter end. She had to endure more lies about herself and a stinging attack from Fitz-Gerald that was sent to the War Office by Dr. Hall. These accusations were the most serious that Florence faced. One of her new friends, Dr. Sutherland, who was a member of Ashley's Sanitary Commission, advised her to write a rebuttal.

Florence preserved her good name, thanks to a man she had never met. The new Secretary of War was now Lord Panmure, and he wanted the truth about Florence and the Army Medical Department. He quietly sent a spy—a Colonel Lefroy—on a secret mission to Constantinople and the Crimea. Lefroy's confidential report cleared Florence of any misconduct, and praised her work in the most glowing way. The new head of the top military command, Sir William Codrington, also sent reports to Lord Panmure praising Florence.

On March 16, 1856, Florence left for the Crimea and her last round with Dr. Hall. The same day a most unusual dispatch arrived in the Crimea. It was written by Lord Panmure himself, and it stated categorically that Florence Nightingale was in command of all the ladies, sisters, and nurses, and that Panmure gave her his confidence and support. He requested that his dispatch be published as part of the general orders of the commander in chief, Sir William. This endorsement from the Cabinet was the greatest triumph that Florence could have. It exceeded her wildest dreams, and it was also an implied censure of Dr. Hall.

Florence arrived at Balaklava on March 24. She was met by Sir William in spite of a raging snowstorm. An attempted reconciliation with Mother Bridgeman failed, and the nun, still defiant of Florence's authority, sailed for home on March 28. On March 30, peace was signed in Paris, but there was no peace for Florence. Dr. Hall and Fitz-Gerald refused food to Florence and her nurses, and they made matters as difficult and unpleasant as possible.

Besides starving her they locked her out of the nurses' hut vacated by Mother Bridgeman. She had to stand in the snow for hours until Dr. Hall relented.

Undaunted, Florence went about her work. She cleaned up the filthy General Hospital and brought relief to the patients. Dr. Hall inspected it and wrote home condemning the conditions in the hospital, stating that it had been much better kept by Mother Bridgeman. Florence was too exhausted to fight back. Hostilities officially ceased on April 29, and one by one the hospitals were closed and the nurses began to go home.

The work in the Crimea was finished by the end of June when Florence returned to Scutari. The last patient left the Barrack Hospital on July 16, 1856, and Florence was free to go. She arranged for all the nurses to be met in London, found them jobs, and gave them money if they needed it. Her praise for the ones who had been a help was unstinted, and even the inadequate ones she refused to have "thrown off like an old shoe."

The British government offered Florence and Aunt Mai a man-of-war ship for a triumphal return home, but they refused. Florence dreaded the bands and the triumphal arches that were being prepared for her. She and her aunt escaped from Constantinople in a small ship, the *Danube*, registering as Mrs. and Miss Smith. Florence left Aunt Mai in Paris and arrived in England alone. She spent a morning in London with some of the nuns who had been her best helpers in Scutari, and then took the afternoon train for Derbyshire. She walked alone from the station to Lea Hurst without being recognized. Then she surprised Fanny, Parthe, and W. E. N. by walking into the drawing room on August 7, 1856.

CHAPTER

IX

Homecoming

The Nightingales had no idea that they were welcoming home a haunted woman. They realized that Florence might have dreadful memories, but they expected that time and the loving atmosphere of home would heal her tired body and spirit. They implored her to rest, to eat well, and to put her war experiences behind her. That was exactly what Florence longed to do. At thirty-six, she felt on the brink of death and she yearned to lay down her head. But she was haunted by the faces of the men who had died, not from battle wounds but from diseases that they had caught in the hospital, diseases that could have been prevented.

The hard lessons learned in the war were already being forgotten or ignored by the War Office. The officials had derived much satisfaction from winning the war, and a thorough whitewashing was given to the officers who had been condemned by the various commissions of inquiry. Dr. Hall was knighted. Florence paced the floors at night, racked by a sense of utter failure.

Florence could not see the fruits of her labor. She did not know that because of her the nurse and the common soldier were transformed in the popular mind into worthy human beings. All she knew was that she had failed to control all the nurses and nuns, that she had antagonized the Army Medical Department, and that many soldiers had returned home to barracks infected with disease that she knew how to prevent.

With bitter tears, Florence decided to devote the rest of her life to improving the lot of the common soldier. She would undertake the reform of the Army Medical Department, even the War Office itself if need be. She would work for the nurses and try to get some proper training for them.

If anything at all was to be achieved, Florence realized that she would have to stifle the popular clamor that surrounded her on her return home. Perhaps she never did fully realize what a heroine she had become, because while she was being toasted in the London clubs and immortalized in popular songs, she had actually been enduring the worst of her humiliations in Scutari and Balaklava.

Fanny had written to her daughter on November 29, 1855: "The most interesting day of thy mother's life. It is very late, my child, but I cannot go to bed without telling you that your meeting had been a glorious one. . . ." The meeting which Fanny described, as well as similar ones held all over England, was called to recognize the work which Florence had done. This particular meeting was held in London. The Duke of Cambridge, a member of the royal family, presided, and the crowd listened to impassioned speeches by Sidney Herbert and Richard Monckton Milnes, among others. The most distinguished guests were then invited to a reception at the Burlington Hotel given by the Nightingales, who had been too overcome to attend the meeting in person.

It was thought at first that Florence would be given a teapot or a bracelet from the donations collected at the various meetings, but so much money came in that it was decided instead to establish a Nightingale Fund. Florence was to be allowed to use this money at her own discretion for the training of nurses. The English soldiers alone contributed over £9,000, and the final total was more than £45,000, a huge sum that was enough to open a school of nursing.

To the people of England Florence was a heroine because she had treated their sons and husbands as human beings. When news of her collapse at Balaklava reached England, the nation mourned, and the soldiers in Scutari wept. When she began to recover, complete strangers spoke the good news to each other in the streets, and the men wept again, this time for joy.

But all of this meant nothing to Florence. Parthe had to answer all but the most important letters, and Florence refused to speak at any meetings or to receive any presents. The faces of the dead dominated her memory, and all the praise only made her feel her failure more acutely.

Florence knew that somehow she had to bring about reforms. In desperation, she wrote to Lord Panmure, but he was away on vacation. Next she wrote to Sidney Her-

bert; he, too, was on vacation. She even wrote to Colonel
Lefroy. She knew that any reforms would have to come
from a man in authority, for the Army Medical Department hated her too thoroughly to accept anything that
came directly from her.

It was Queen Victoria who finally came to the rescue.
She wanted to hear about the war firsthand from Florence,
so Sir James Clark, the Queen's physician, invited Florence to Scotland in September for a short vacation. Within
three days of her arrival, Florence was a guest at Balmoral
Castle, where the Queen vacationed.

The two women liked each other immediately. They
established a rapport that enabled Florence to ask the
Queen for what she wanted, namely a royal commission to
examine the Army Medical Department. The Queen sent
for Lord Panmure and introduced Florence to him, com-
mending her ideas. Later, Lord Panmure agreed to set up
the commission as Florence outlined it, and he also agreed
to accept a confidential report from Florence.

At the beginning of November the Nightingales took
up residence in the Burlington Hotel in London. Florence's friends came to call it "the little War Office," as she
lay there on her sofa and received important visitors.

When Lord Panmure came to call, he brought with him
a draft of the composition of the royal commission. Florence had her own draft ready and they discussed the
matter for three hours. In the end they agreed that Sidney
Herbert should be chairman of the commission. Florence
also persuaded Lord Panmure to accept Sir James Clark,
Dr. Sutherland, and Augustus Stafford, but she failed to
get Colonel Lefroy.

Although Florence was greatly excited by this new development, she soon realized that nothing was happening. Christmas came and went. Months passed, and still nothing happened. Finally, Florence resorted to threats. She assured Lord Panmure that if he did not proceed with the royal commission she would publish an account of all her experiences in the Crimea and expose the entire Army Medical Department. The threat worked, aided by the pressure brought to bear by Sidney Herbert.

At last, in April, 1857, Lord Panmure brought the official draft to the Burlington Hotel. Although he tried to include a list of unsuitable personnel, Florence insisted and got her own way. On May 5, the royal warrant was issued, and Sidney Herbert called the commissioners together within the week.

Florence and Herbert worked well together. She stayed behind the scenes, quietly supplying all the details, while Herbert handled public relations and persuaded important people to support the cause. Florence came to know every witness personally, and coached them in what they had to say. She became friends with all the commissioners, even Dr. Sutherland. Although he sacrificed his career to work for Florence—for nothing—she rewarded him with scoldings and more work. They passionately believed in the same things, but she could scarcely conceal the fact that he irritated her to death.

In June, Dr. Hall was called before the commission. This was the perfect opportunity for revenge, but Florence asked that he not be harassed by the questions. The work was too important for personal feelings to interfere with it. When it came time for Florence to testify, she decided to submit a report in writing. Her evidence was contained in thirty closely written pages.

The summer of 1857 was unusually hot. Florence worked at the Burlington Hotel, keeping two projects going at once. She wrote *Notes on Matters Affecting the Health, Efficiency, and Hospital Administration of the British Army*, which ran to more than a thousand pages, and at the same time she worked on the report of the royal commission. Fanny and Parthe complained about the heat but refused to leave Florence alone. They were noisy and inconsiderate, and as usual found Florence's behavior incomprehensible.

A new worry now began to aggravate Florence. She suspected that when the report was given to Lord Panmure, he would sit back with a sigh of relief and do nothing about it. She gave him a copy of her *Notes*, and he set it aside, unread. After another conference with Herbert, they presented Panmure with highlights from the report. Herbert tactfully proposed that the most glaring abuses be remedied right away to avoid a public scandal. Florence went back to work. If precise plans were not laid out for implementing her ideas, the report would certainly be a dead issue.

Florence designed four subcommittees to carry out the work recommended in the report. Each committee would have a chairman with executive powers and an interim grant from the Treasury. One subcommittee would put all army barracks in order and revise their sanitary arrangements. Another would begin a statistical department for the army. A third would start an army medical school, and a fourth would revamp the Army Medical Department from top to bottom.

By August 11, Florence had a complete collapse, and was taken to a resort town in the Midlands. W. E. N. went to see her and said that she was dying. It was Aunt Mai, not Fanny, who went to her rescue.

When Florence was well enough to travel, she and Aunt Mai went back to London. Florence now made out her will, leaving her entire fortune to build a model barracks which included a section for families. She also continued to work on the detailed plans for the four committees. Lord Panmure went to Scotland for another vacation, but he could not escape from Florence. Now she applied pressure through the newspapers. Without any mention of her name, various articles appeared, written by Herbert and others, in support of the reforms she urged. She even wrote an anonymous pamphlet, called *Mortality in the British Army*. It was a graphic work, believed to be the first in which charts were used to show statistical data.

By now frightened, Lord Panmure gave in by the end of the year. In December, 1857, he established the four subcommittees exactly as Florence wished. The new year began well. Aunt Mai took over the management of Florence's housekeeping affairs in the annex of the Burlington Hotel. At last, her family began to leave her alone.

Parthe was to be married that year, and she and Fanny became very occupied with wedding preparations. Her prospective husband, Sir Henry Verney, was a fifty-six-year-old widower who had first proposed to Florence. After her marriage, Parthe became a changed woman, and she was able to effect a genuine reconciliation with Florence over the years.

Marianne Nicholson, who was now Mrs. Douglas Galton, also renewed her friendship with Florence, although the two women had little left in common. Galton became a member of the Barrack subcommittee. An expert engineer, he specialized in heating, ventilation, drains, and water supply, and became an invaluable aide to Florence.

Many notables found their way to the door of the Burlington Hotel, including royalty and important government officials. A debate in the House of Commons, in May, 1858, on the health of the army produced results that were most favorable to Florence's cause. However, by autumn she decided to use the press again and to do a little private politicking. Copies of her *Notes* were printed and distributed to Cabinet members, officials at the War Office, and even the Queen.

One of Florence's acquaintances was a very unusual woman called Harriet Martineau. Harriet was an editorial writer for the *Daily News*, a position never before held by a woman. She used a copy of the *Notes* that Florence sent her for a series of articles called "England and Her Soldiers." They were well received and gave Florence just the right amount of anonymous publicity that she needed.

The work of the four subcommittees proceeded. That year a model kitchen was opened in Wellington barracks in London by Alexis Soyer, the cook from Scutari.

Soyer died in August, 1858, and shortly after that Florence's chief associate and helper, Sidney Herbert, became fatally ill. However, Florence refused to recognize that he was dying and she goaded him into new efforts for their "cause." Accusing him of laziness, she declared that she was dying, too.

Herbert endured Florence's bitter attacks with sweetness and resignation. His wife, Liz, seemed to be on Florence's side, and kept urging him to greater efforts. Already doing more than he should, he suddenly was given the chairmanship of another very important committee. The year before there had been a mutiny against Britain in India. Although Florence had wanted to go and nurse the British troops, her health had prevented her. Instead, she was able to get a "Royal Commission to Enquire into the Health of the British Army in India." The commission was set up in 1859, with Herbert as chairman. In March of that year, a change of government brought Lord Palmerston back as prime minister, and the new head of the War Office was, of course, Sidney Herbert.

When Florence heard the news she was ecstatic. At last, all they had hoped for and dreamed about could now come true. But her joy was short-lived. When the machinery of the War Office, in all its incredible convolutions, became clear to her, she knew that everything she had worked for could be destroyed by administrative red tape. She would just have to reform the War Office. There was little pleasure or excitement in her labors now, for Herbert was becoming more and more crushed by his burdens, and he longed to return to his country home.

In the summer of 1859, Florence collapsed again, but this time Aunt Mai had to tend to her own family, who were complaining bitterly of neglect. Hilary Bonham-Carter stayed with Florence in Hampstead until Aunt Mai's return that October. But Aunt Mai could not sacrifice her own family forever, and she finally left Florence in 1860. For nearly twenty years, Florence refused to speak to her.

Although Hilary returned, even Florence realized that

Hilary was wasting her life by devoting it to her. So she drove her away a few months before Sidney Herbert died, on August 2, 1861. Now Florence felt that her usefulness was at an end. They had failed. The greatest opportunity of a lifetime had been lost. Sidney's last words had been: "Poor Florence, our joint work unfinished."

Florence's friendship with both the Herberts had been one of the great joys of her life. After Sidney's death, she and Liz remained close friends.

CHAPTER

✠✠✠✠✠✠✠✠✠

X

✠✠✠✠✠✠✠✠✠

An Invalid's Work

Although the British soldier was uppermost in her thoughts when she returned from the Crimea, Florence did not forget her nurses. In 1859, she wrote a book called *Notes on Hospitals*. It was an expert treatise on the construction of hospitals and how they should be run. Florence remained a consultant on hospital planning for many years, and had a hand in the design of numbers of hospitals in England. Fresh air and sunshine for patients were still considered harmful by some medical practitioners, but Florence was instrumental in overcoming this idea.

She advocated the construction of wards with adequate space between the beds. She wanted clean, spacious kitchens and laundry rooms. She gave instructions for glass or earthenware cups, hair mattresses, and iron bedsteads, all things which could be cleaned easily. She asked for pale pink walls instead of the dark green ones that were the standard of the day. She studied drains and statistics, and produced model forms for record keeping. She even invented a new system for classifying diseases.

In December, 1860, *Notes on Nursing* was published, and rapidly became a best seller. Its effect was incalculable, not only because of its great good sense and practical information, but because Florence had become a popular legend, and women from all walks of life were prepared to believe what she said. The book shows Florence at her best. It is witty and racy, and still is amusing reading today, unlike her other writings. The later editions include a section called "Minding Baby."

In *Notes on Nursing*, Florence displayed great insight into the mental attitudes of sick people. Sensitive to their worries and their loneliness, she had a talent for easing both mind and body. "Apprehension, uncertainty, waiting, expectation, fear of surprise, do a patient more harm than any exertion. Remember he is face to face with his enemy all the time, internally wrestling with him, having long imaginary conversations with him. You are thinking of something else." She described many details of practical nursing and hygiene for the home. The book was sold in the United States, and was translated into most European languages.

Florence solved the problem of what to do with the Nightingale Fund money in 1859, when she decided to open a nursing school at St. Thomas's Hospital in London. The governors of the hospital had asked her advice about plans for a major rebuilding, and as a result they had purchased land in the borough of Lambeth. Her contact with the hospital personnel was so pleasant that Florence de-

cided to start her school there. The matron, a Mrs. Ward-
roper, was an unusually fine woman, and Florence knew
she would have to rely on her heavily, since her own condition would not permit her to take an active part in running
the school.

The doctors at St. Thomas's did not want the school of
nursing on their premises. They dismissed nurses' training
as sheer nonsense, with the exception of Mr. Whitfield,
the resident medical officer, who gave the school his un-
qualified support. (In England, when a doctor achieves
specialist status he drops the title "Doctor" and reverts to
Mister.)

The leader of the opposition was Mr. South, the senior
consulting surgeon. In his mind, nurses were fit only to
scrub floors, and he wanted to keep all the care and treatment of patients in the hands of the doctors.

Opposition or no, Florence started her school, based on
two principles. One, nurses' training should be carried out
only in well-organized hospitals; and two, nurses should
live in pleasant surroundings in a nurses' home where they
could be carefully supervised. The initial aim of the school
was to produce nurses who could train others. The first
class, begun in June, 1860, had an enrollment of fifteen
students for the one-year course.

The young women were selected with utmost care, for
on them rested the success or failure of the experiment.
Florence still had to fight the reputation that clung to the
word "nurse." The few women who were chosen had to
have impeccable moral characters. Any flirtation would
result in instant dismissal, as would a date with a medical
student. The girls were allowed out only in pairs, neatly

dressed in brown uniforms and white caps, and aprons.

Florence set up an elaborate system of marking. Besides lecture notebooks and practical instruction in the wards being marked, the girls' behavior was graded, too. They were scored on their punctuality, personal appearance, manners, and even the way they kept their bureau drawers. Each student had a tastefully furnished room to herself. The pleasant sitting room contained books and maps and fresh flowers sent by the absent Miss Nightingale.

It seemed hard to realize that Florence was not there in person, working with the girls, for she thoroughly supervised from her sofa. The girls came to see her, and she insisted that they keep a personal diary that she could read. She also corrected any spelling errors. When the year ended, applications for the services of the fledgling nurses poured in from all over England.

In 1861, money from the Nightingale Fund was used to establish a school for the training of midwives. These women, mostly from rural areas, were given a six-month course. Florence insisted that they be decently housed and properly supervised so that respectable women would not hesitate to make the journey to London. The school was successful, and resulted in better care for mothers and newborn babies.

It is difficult to understand how Florence was able to handle the volume of work that passed through her hands. While she was working, she was still concerned about philosophy and religion. She had rebelled against the Church of England in her Harley Street days, but always considered herself a woman of deep personal faith. God was very real to her, and some of her lifelong struggle to express her religious ideas is contained in her book *Suggestions for Thought*. She rewrote it later, in spite of her overwhelming burden of work.

In April, 1861, the Civil War broke out in the United States, and in October the Secretary at War in Washington asked Florence for advice on hospital organization and care of the wounded. She corresponded with Miss Dorothea Dix, Superintendent of Nurses for the Union armies, and supplied her with detailed information. At the end of the war, Florence received an official letter of thanks from the Secretary of the United States Christian Union.

In England, the ambitious reform of the War Office, scarcely begun by Sidney Herbert, ended with his death. Florence succeeded in getting Douglas Galton promoted, but she was depressed to find that he could not succeed where Sidney Herbert had failed. Florence was unable to work with Sir George Lewis, the new head of the War Office. When he was eventually succeeded by Lord de Grey, whom Florence could trust, she no longer pressed for complete reorganization. She used her remaining influence to improve the sanitary conditions of barracks and military hospitals, and to harass the Army Medical Department.

Florence had always been greatly concerned with the British army in India, and she could not stay out of the investigation of the condition of troops there. She suspected that all kinds of unsanitary conditions existed and that needless deaths occurred, but when she made inquiries she was told that there was no available information. So Florence drafted a "circular of inquiry," and sent it to every military station in India. Between 1859 and 1862, she analyzed the returns with the help of Dr. Sutherland. This sick woman, growing old and long grown sad, had become one of Britain's leading India experts without ever getting out of bed.

The "Station Reports," as the returns came to be called, revealed a grim picture, filling the second volume of the report of the Indian Sanitary Commission, almost one thousand pages. Florence was not allowed to give evidence before the commissioners, so she submitted *Observations* in writing.

However, enemies at the India Office suppressed the evidence. The original report was available to members of Parliament only, not to the public. The report concerned dirt and contaminated water, mud floors, heat, and overcrowding in barracks and hospitals. But Florence was even more appalled by what she learned about Indian villagers. Her attempts to help them were defeated because civil and military administrations were separated in India. She raged against the authority that not only permitted such misery but was actively opposed to alleviating it.

Florence had the report printed at her own expense and sent to every army officer in India. She also launched a publicity campaign in *The Times*.

The recommendations of the India Sanitary Commission were flexible enough for Florence to begin writing a program for their implementation. After the death of Lord Elgin, the Viceroy of India, in October, 1863, his successor, Sir John Lawrence, took an unprecedented step by coming to see Florence on December 4. She had been influential in getting him the appointment, and he trusted her knowledge and her judgment. Lawrence had spent most of his life in India, and had been governor of the Punjab during the Indian Mutiny.

By January, 1864, Florence had completed her *Suggestions in Regard to Sanitary Works required for the Improvement of Indian Stations*. After having copies printed and sent to India, she waited hopefully, but nothing happened. Lawrence, unfortunately, did not turn out to be the best viceroy that India would ever have, and he was soon crushed by his responsibilities. Army doctors in India were able to defeat a proposal to introduce nurses on a limited scale.

After this setback, a new friendship raised Florence's hopes again. Sir Stratford Northcote was now the Secretary of State for India, and he, too, came to seek her advice. At her suggestion, he set up a Department of Public Health for India, and Florence supplied him with a digest of the whole Indian sanitary affair from 1859 to 1867. At Florence's prompting, he requested annual reports from India, and at last things began to get done.

Along with her work for India, Florence continued to press for the improvement of public health standards in England. One of the many requests for nurses came from William Rathbone in Liverpool. He wanted to provide free nursing for the poor in his part of the country, especially by having a district nurse help people in their own homes rather than in a hospital. With Florence's assistance, Rathbone opened a nursing school in Liverpool. She kept in contact with him as he developed his work to include nursing for inmates of the local workhouse.

Of all the brutal treatment given to paupers in the nineteenth century, perhaps the worst was at a workhouse in-

firmary. To Florence, it was Scutari all over again. Her
rage was fanned by the death, through gross neglect, of a
pauper called Timothy Dale. Florence offered nurses to
the London Poor Law Board, and began an inquiry into
Dale's death. She circulated a "form of enquiry" to every
workhouse infirmary in the country.

Florence sent a team of twelve nurses and a matron to
William Rathbone to tackle the worst infirmary in Liverpool. The head of the team was Agnes Jones, an heiress, a
niece of Sir John Lawrence, and a graduate of the Nightingale School of Nursing and the Kaiserwerth Institution
in Germany. Miss Jones left for Liverpool in May, 1865.
She died on February 19, 1868, of typhus that she caught
from her patients, her condition aggravated by overwork in
filth, danger, and misery.

Florence knew that it would take an Act of Parliament to
reform the care of the destitute sick, and she fought for
workhouse reform and a new Poor Law for London. But
the inadequate Act of Parliament of March, 1867, left her
cold with rage.

Inadequate as it was, the act did remove all children, as
well as two thousand cases of insanity, from the work-
houses. The sick were accommodated in separate buildings,
and the salaries of medical personnel were now paid out of
a central fund instead of being dependent on local parish
rates. A start was also made to improve some of the incredible buildings where the destitute were housed.

In 1867, Florence found another outlet for her energies.
She had had to close her midwives' school because of an
outbreak of fever among the new mothers, and she began
to search for reasons why so many babies died. The re-

search took three years, aided by Dr. Sutherland, who helped her to complete *Introductory Notes on Lying-in Institutions,* in 1871. Florence recommended separate rooms for the mothers, rather than the huge wards then in use.

Although Florence fought for the rights of nurses, she did not think that women should become doctors. Neither did she join the suffragette movement or campaign for women's rights. Using herself as an example, she declared that any woman who was prepared to work hard could get anyplace she wanted.

This was an unfair approach, and gradually Florence came to realize it. Her own achievements had stemmed directly from her social position and her wealth, without which she would probably have achieved nothing.

CHAPTER

✸✸✸✸✸✸✸✸✸

XI

✸✸✸✸✸✸✸✸✸

The Declining Years

For ten years after her return from Constantinople, Florence had labored incessantly. She kept an incredible number of schemes going at once, while her health became progressively worse. Much of her problem was emotional, and staying in bed seemed a marvelous way to prevent interruptions to her work. Her family was intimidated by her threat that she was going to die at any moment, and so they left her alone.

Florence had become all mind and will, with a disposition so caustic that it was no wonder her family avoided her and her friends stayed away. She hated to see people and kept her happiest relationships through letters. One of the few people with whom she maintained a cordial correspondence was Benjamin Jowett, a professor at Oxford University.

Everything had to be sacrificed to her work, which she felt was of tremendous importance. If she did not do it, it would not get done. Never satisfied with her accomplishments, she expected dramatic results. Along with a tendency for self-dramatization, she considered herself a very important person.

Florence now lived alone with her servants, in the heart of fashionable London. W. E. N. had bought her the house in October, 1865, declaring that her expensive lodgings were too much for him. Without a companion, she suffered from loneliness despite her work. But she was consoled by her cats, who were allowed the freedom of her bedroom, and they amused her with their antics. She also began to study Greek again.

The bedroom at South Street was sunny, and it overlooked a garden. An immaculate housekeeper, Florence kept a firm hand on her servants, giving them very precise instructions. She received visitors one at a time, and would see no one without an appointment, not even a house guest.

It now became obvious that Florence's health was failing, and her family persuaded her to pay them a visit. So, in the summer of 1868, Florence, now forty-eight years old, went to Lea Hurst for three months. She had not been there since her return from Constantinople in 1856.

When Florence returned to London she tried to continue her work, but, by 1872, even she was forced to admit that she had "gone out of office." Her last plans were the foundations of the British Red Cross Aid Society, giving instructions on every aspect of the care of the sick. She also raised money and sent help to the victims of the Franco-Prussian War of 1870.

In 1872, Fanny and W. E. N., no longer able to manage their affairs, sent for Florence. She spent eight months at

Embley trying to sort things out, and hated every minute of it. She longed to return to London to be near her nursing school. Perhaps the main reason was that she had gradually shed her burden of administrative work, and had begun to indulge her love of company. Some of her closest companions were the nurses, whose gossip kept her in touch with the outside world.

W. E. N. died on January 10, 1874. According to his will, Aunt Mai was to inherit the bulk of the Nightingale fortune, which included the estate of Embley Park. But the family had spent most of their lives there, so Florence asked Aunt Mai to allow Fanny to live there until she died. Aunt Mai refused. It took until July to disentangle Fanny from Embley. Fanny was now blind and her mind was failing. Florence moved her out of Embley Park and cared for her until her death in 1880.

Parthe became ill, too, and the sisters were close again until Parthe died in 1890. Uncle Sam had died in 1881, and Florence was reconciled with Aunt Mai.

With her family wounds healed, Florence seemed to become her old self again. But suddenly she was called back to work. The government asked her to take part in an inquiry into the neglect of wounded soldiers in Egypt. The doors of the War Office opened to hear her opinion, and, wonder of wonders, she found herself on cordial terms with the Army Medical Department. A group of nurses was sent to Egypt by the government. It was a victory at last. Florence felt so much better that she rose from her bed and went to the Nightingale School of Nursing. She was also encouraged by success in India, where many of the measures she had advocated were adopted. By 1888, there was a sanitary board in every province.

During the next few years, Florence's work began to bear fruit. Many schools of nursing were established after her pattern, and Nightingale-trained nurses went to many parts of the world.

After 1896 Florence never left her bedroom, and by 1901 she was totally blind. In 1907, Florence was awarded the Order of Merit, the first woman to receive this decoration. In 1910, the Freedom of the City of London was conferred upon her. She died that year, on August 13, at the age of ninety.

In a letter dated New Year's Eve, 1879, Benjamin Jowett had written to Florence:

There was a great deal of romantic feeling about you twenty-three years ago when you came home from the Crimea. (I really believe that you might have been a Duchess if you had played your cards better!) And now you work on in silence, and nobody knows how many lives are saved by your nurses in hospitals (you have introduced a new era in nursing): how many thousands of soldiers who would have fallen victims to bad air, bad drainage and ventilation, are now alive owing to your forethought and diligence; how many natives of India in this generation and in generations to come have been preserved from famine, oppression and the load of debt by the energy of a sick lady who can scarcely rise from her bed. The world does not know all this, or think about it. But I know it and often think about it, and I want you to, so that in the later years of your course you may see what a blessed life yours is and has been.

Chronology

1820 Florence Nightingale born, Florence, Italy, May 12.

1837 Receives "call from God" to serve Him, February 7; Nightingales travel on the Continent, September.

1839 Nightingales return to London. Florence and her sister are presented to Queen Victoria.

1840 Florence is introduced to Lord Ashley and Lord Palmerston.

1842 Florence is introduced to the Prussian Ambassador to London; meets Richard Monckton Milnes.

1845 Refuses to marry Henry Nicholson. Announces plan to train as a nurse and is refused permission by her outraged family.

1847 The Bracebridges take Florence to Rome where she meets Sidney Herbert.

1848   Refuses to marry Richard Monckton Milnes.

1850   Works at Kaiserwerth, Germany.

1851   Returns to Kaiserwerth.

1853   Reorganizes the Institution for the Care of Sick
         Gentlewomen, in Harley Street.

1854   Crimean War breaks out. Florence leads party
         of nuns and nurses to Constantinople. Allies
         land in the Crimea, September 12. Battle of the
         River Alma, September 20. Battle of Balaklava,
         October 25. Battle of Inkerman, Florence arrives
         in Scutari, November 5.

1855   Fall of Sebastopol, September 8.

1856   Florence commended in General Orders of the
         British army, March 16. Arrives home, August
         7.

1857   Royal Commission on the Health of the Army is
         formed.

1858   Florence moves to annex of the Burlington
         Hotel.

1859   The Royal Commission on the Health of the
         Army in India is formed. Nightingale School of
         Nursing opens at St. Thomas's Hospital.

1861   Florence sets up school for the training of mid-
         wives. Gives advice to America for the care of
         the wounded during the Civil War.

1865   Florence sends Agnes Jones to Liverpool to re-
         form the Workhouse Infirmary.

1867   Investigates diseases in maternity.

1872   Takes over management of parents' affairs.

1874   W. E. N. dies.

1880   Frances (Fanny) dies.

1890   Parthe dies.

1896   Florence retires to her bedroom until her death.

1907   Awarded the Order of Merit.

1910   Given the Freedom of the City of London.

1910   Florence Nightingale dies, August 13.

Some Writings of Florence Nightingale

The Institution of Kaiserwerth on the Rhine for the Practical Training of Deaconesses. 1851

Letters from Egypt. 1854

Statements Exhibiting the Voluntary Contributions Received by Miss Nightingale for the Use of British Hospitals in the East. 1858

Notes on Matters Affecting the Health, Efficiency, and Hospital Administration of the British Army. 1858

Subsidiary Notes as to the Introduction of Female Nursing into Military Hospitals in Peace and in War. 1858

A Contribution to the Sanitary History of the British Army During the Late War with Russia. 1859

Notes on Hospitals. 1859 (Rewritten in 1863)

Suggestions for Thought. 1860

Notes on Nursing. 1860

Army Sanitary Administration and Its Reform under the Late Lord Herbert. 1862.

Observations. 1863

Introductory Notes on Lying–In Institutions. 1871

Life or Death in India. 1873

On Trained Nursing for the Sick Poor. 1876

Miss Florence Nightingale's Addresses to Probationer-Nurses. 1872–1900

Florence Nightingale's Indian Letters. 1878–1882 (Some of these were published, some printed privately.)

Suggestions for Further Reading

Gibbs, Peter. *Crimean Blunder*. New York: Holt, Rinehart and Winston, 1960.

Strachey, Lytton. *Eminent Victorians*. New York: G. P. Putnam's Sons, 1918.

Woodham-Smith, Cecil. *Florence Nightingale*. New York: McGraw-Hill, 1951.

Index

115